The Polk Street Review

#historymatters

2023 edition
a global anthology
published in Noblesville, IN

Community
Education
Arts
Press

First Printing: February 2023

Editors: Alys Caviness-Gober & Sarah E. Morin
Cover design: Alys Caviness-Gober
Cover art: *Wave* by Alys Caviness-Gober
Additional *Art Nouveau* images provided by Alys Caviness-Gober
Project design, formatting, and layout: Alys Caviness-Gober

ISBN: 978-0-9998858-8-8

Community • Education • Arts Press
a division of *Community • Education • Arts, Inc.*
Noblesville, IN 46060
1st Printing: February 2023
https://CEArts.org

Ordering Information:
Please contact at info@cearts.org for details.

dedicated to our families and friends

Individual Sponsors

David Allen
John Caviness
Alys Caviness-Gober
Bonita Cox Searle
Jerry Dreesen
Chuck Kellum
Sarah E. Morin
Jean Roberts

Thank you to all who support CEArts!

Table of Contents

Introduction

Through recent challenging times, *The Polk Street Review* remains what it always was: a place to celebrate writers and artists. We are a community as much as a publication, reaching beyond Noblesville, Indiana as we receive submissions from all over the world, and for the past several years, we have encouraged our more local submitters to think globally. This year, we have again woven global-minded pieces throughout the body of the anthology. You will see a globe symbol 🌎 when either the subject matter of a piece steps outside our own community or was sent by a creator outside the United States.

As editors, we try to clarify meaning or fix an odd capitalization here or there, but our goal has always been not to tamper too much with the voice of the writer. Except when we felt necessary, we have chosen to respect our contributor's artistic choices. Sometimes that means publishing pieces with viewpoints very different from our own. Sometimes we have updated language to reflect what we see as best modern inclusive practice, and sometimes we have chosen to let verbiage stand in historical pieces. We hope we have struck the balance in any published pieces between respecting the intent of the author and being responsible as a culturally sensitive organization. Inclusion is one of our core values at CEArts, and we have learned our own journey in that process is ever evolving. We beg forgiveness for any editorial interference that left too much said or too much unsaid.

We have again selected award winners in each of the following categories: *Poetry and Lyrics*, *Prose*, and *Artwork Images*. The selection process is both a joy and a job. How are we to choose between so many excellent pieces when all deserve recognition? After much discussion, we select pieces in each category that stand out to us, in our own subjective opinions. We applaud these artists and writers for their high degree of craftsmanship and creativity, and invite you to view the list of winners at the back of the book. Please note two additional awards: *Special Award* and *Award of Merit*. A *Special Award* goes to one or more contributors who have given *The Polk Street Review* something that cannot be captured by the other prizes, but deserves recognition. The *Award of Merit* is our highest honor: it is our selected "Best in Book" out of all submitted pieces.

This year, our optional theme is a hashtag: *#historymatters*. It feels particularly relevant amidst the ongoing global pandemic and today's cultural and political climate here and abroad. At *CEArts*, we're doing what we can to answer the call of history, offering an array of inclusive arts opportunities and projects for creatives of all kinds to share their work. *The Polk Street Review* is one of those projects. We're grateful to our sponsors and to the people who sent us their wonderful creations. We hope you as a reader enjoy your time spent here in our community of artists and writers.

The Things We Love To Do

at

CEArts

based in
Noblesville, Indiana

CEArts.org

Cleaning Out The Attic by Noble Poets

My family traces its history,
faded as tissue-thin paper;
there on the page,
written over a hundred years ago
on the back of a daguerreotype,
handwritten, but without a signature,
wisps of spidery ink trailing and
telling a tale of people I never knew,
yet here they are,
the age-gapped wedded bliss
of Uncle Joe (groom at forty-two)
and Aunt Doris (bride at twenty-one)
on their Silver Anniversary,
his white-haired frailty as apparent as
her caring hand resting tenderly on his shoulder,
his right hand around her waist
left sleeve folded up for his phantom limb.

Joe left her side, and for more than 30 years
other photographs show she
always dressed in widow's weeds,
sometimes sharing a soft smile,
never complaining about the loneliness
yet not whole;

a love captured in time
promised to each other
a love prevailed through the years.

(*Noble Poets* poetry group contributors: Alys Caviness-Gober,
David Allen, Mike Nierste, Chuck Kellum, and Z. Rose)

12

Character by Sarah E. Morin

We want the vote!
We want the vote!

My bustle bounces a militant jig as I lead the parade of elementary girls, three stroller moms, and one hip Baby Boomer grandma, pressed white slacks marching in rhythm. Fathers confine themselves to the sidelines, cell phones extended. Are they holding the feminism at arm's length? Or preserving the moment for Facebook, caption: *Vacation at the History Museum?* A stray grandpa hollers for us to go back to the kitchen. Engage or let it slide? My 19th-Century self is torn. The twinkle in his creased eye says he's playing but I wonder how his eight-year-old granddaughter hears it, carrying one end of the tasseled banner that trumpets VOTES FOR WOMEN. But I'm glad I have an opponent as I haul myself onto the wobbly soapbox. My speech is impassioned, and without Old Man Heckler playing his improvised role, I would have nothing to push against. For every 3rd grade girl and her mom agrees we need the vote, but none are able to tell me why. Would our foremothers be proud or frustrated that the right denied them is now so normal we take it for granted?

We want the vote!
We want –

Want (verb): lacking a thing necessary to completeness.

We want--
Want –

Want (noun): being without the necessities of life; destitution; poverty.

What does hunger mean to the belly that is full?

I want to *want* something as soul-deep as these women did. I try to summon the hollow-chest war cry from my corseted belly. "I want the vote!" A high-pitched voice chirps, "Me too!" There is no hashtag in her voice, but I want to convey to these comfortable sunhat vacationers that the vote was our great-great-grandmothers' #MeToo. Divisive. Visceral. Personal. Inspiring admiration, rage, mockery. They see me as a comical character from *Mary Poppins* when I see myself as Susan B. Anthony. How many of us on this close-cropped Victorian lawn voted in the last election? Did I? I think Hip Grandma must--she carries herself like she tooth-and-nailed her way to VP of some small corporation, the sole drop of stubborn estrogen in a testosterone-soaked boardroom. She'd make the better suffragette. I shout defiance to a world I know already agrees with me. My bravery is sewn on. I want to make Aunt Susan proud, but my character is 9 to 5. I know all the historic facts about these women but I don't know their struggle. I sip the injustice of their lives like a sour wine: taste, analyze, spit out, then go back to my iced Diet Coke at the end of the work day.

I want –

My button-up boots from the costume room pinch.

Street Names by Ndaba Sibanda

Voyager Thabi had seen it all,
She had travelled far and wide
and experienced a series of shocks
cuisines, music, colors, and climates.

Not only had she had the privilege
and honor of visiting several countries
on this earth, she also set foot on other
planets, her eyes on extraterrestrials.

If there were inscriptions on her
forehead, maybe the words would
read like: *culture shock no longer
shocks me, I just stunned it big time.*

She had come across individuals
who named their kids after books,
for instance, one boy was Dictionary,
little wonder, his teacher used to say:
Dictionary, give me the meaning of this.

She had seen medical bodies or institutes
with eyebrow-raising names, too, for example,
one of them was called *Prestigious Psychological
Menopause School of Sciences and Signs*, wow!

On another planet, she was captivated
by street names like: *Is Lyfe A Beach?
Naught In Anoder Lyfe, Fool Stop, Go
To Eel or Earth, Full Me Thri-c I'm Yo Full!*

*I thout U Where My Half, Why DD
U Leve Me, What Hapend? Riched
A Dad End, My Everytin, U I Mine,
Go Bed They Will Defurther U, C U.*

*U Wested My Tyme, Which Me Luck,
Which U Da Beast! Sory Waz Rong,
Miss U 2 March, Com Bake Darlie,
4eve Yoz, Gud Tymz We Heard 2.*

Thabi discovered that aliens
named the city's streets after
their break-ups or fallouts,
or issues with their exes.

She learned that the street name:
Go Bed They Will Defurther U,
actually means: *Go bird, they
will defeather you ahead.*

Light by Vivianne Belle

before the harshness of electricity
candles offered a softer light
and perhaps we missed the opportunity
to see each more gently

Alone with this rambling mind by Alison Harlos

Alienation
Beats devastation anyway
Alone with my take on today
Yesterday
Last week
4 years ago.
I'm not hiding from you
I'm just processing. Things.
So I ask to be left alone
Please don't leave me
Behind
While my mind is processing. Things.
Ring me up. Ask me over. Touch my hand. Expect a stare,
And a smile
You're still there?
Grateful
I've been hiding from. Things. Still chewing on. Things.
Ring me up. Ask me over, say you need my attention, I'll bend over for
you.

The Poet by Chuck Kellum

I cast words
To the wind
Not knowing
Where they'll land:
Perhaps upon your doorstep,
Perhaps into your hand.

And then into your mind,
Or deep within your heart,
So you and I may meet (again?),
Though long and far apart.

Battered Paint Can by Kenneth Conklin

The old man holds a
battered paint can.
Like the paint can,
the old man
Has some dents.
And his top is loose,
but there's still
a bit of paint
within the can.
Just like there's yet
some life in the man.
Who reaches for
a battered brush
and with his gnarled hand
swipes a few strokes
of bright color
to brighten his
his old dark room.

Taking the Opportunity: A Steuben County Poem by Nancy Simmonds

When Gunther was sent north to work in the parks
he knew nothin' but city cars and streets, gambling and hunger.
The CCC gave him three squares, five bucks in pocket money
and twenty-five sent back, to keep his sister home

if she'd listen. The trees were tall and dark, silent
as a bread line crowd. The sky was big, full of birds and stars
not one empty building to hide them from sight. The deep lake
had some tasty fish and the air smelled clean. He felt rich.

The fellas were mostly fine, willing to put their backs into
the job and get it done right. He worked moving rock,
splitting logs, building trails and shelters. Hands sap sticky
he planted rows and rows and rows of trees. Every dawn call you could
see

the difference they all made. It was good.

17

At mail call some would share stories from home, grateful words
they all needed to hear. The silence, the not-knowing
was the worst. He made up bad things in the night. Then

Herman and the Jinx Brothers got it in their heads to build
the toboggan run Ollie had been yapping about in the old country.
Sarge let them have at it and in a few weeks of after hours and
weekends
they were slip sliding down that track faster than any fliver
or racehorse could go. Gunther wrote Sis all about it.

He never heard back.

Excerpts from *Journey to the West 1840* by Jean Roberts

Editor's Note: The following is a work of historical fiction.

Onto The Canal Boat

In Toledo, the Wabash-Erie Canal ran right next to downtown, so it
was easy for us to transport our baggage into an overnight hotel and
then proceed on to the canal boat the next morning. After buying our
tickets we proceeded onto a packet boat equipped for passengers
headed west. The boats were something like 40 feet long and 10 feet
across, and brightly painted to contrast with the green spring landscape
they travelled through.

There were freight and passenger packets. Smaller boats could be
outfitted for shorter trips. Larger passenger packets consisted of a series
of rooms along the length. Towards the front was the main saloon,
where meals were taken, provided by the crew and part of your ticket.
The boats stop traveling nightly; the horses need to rest, and it's not
safe for them to walk the towpaths in the dark. Boats depart an hour
after dawn, and make daily stops at noon and an hour before dark. They
put in at docks constructed along the way, where there are small
settlements with traders and always some small inns, offering
accommodations. Or, passengers can stay overnight on the boat, where
the front and rear rooms get converted into overnight sleeping rooms
for men and women respectively.

Our trip to Peru on the canal was about 170 miles long, and would take
between three and four days, thus possibly four overnights. I expected

that we would prefer the inns, but we decided to wait and see. On the boat there was also a small chamber for toileting, the arrangement was rather rude. I was glad I wore a narrow skirt. There was a temptation to not drink any water because of the difficulty of elimination, although I knew this to not be healthful.

Many kinds of people were lined up to board the few packets docked. I saw mostly men looking for work, on canal projects in Indiana or on farms; some were traders and merchants, taking their wares west to sell, and then traveling east again with other materials to sell. There were also some small families; couples, and couples with a child, looking to start a new life. Hungry looking people. Due the recent economic collapse of 1837, we also saw some former elites (evident by the quality of their clothing); they were also hungry and anxious for opportunity. We loaded early in the morning after a short breakfast. We found stowage under the seat for our luggage. We settled on the hard benches and began long hours of watching green foliage slowly travel by and waiting for the scanty lunch service. There was a little conversation, but that quieted as the hours dragged on.

After the first long day, we docked at some tiny settlement in the woods and had to face the question: Staying on the boat? Staying at the inn? The inn was made of crude buildings just recently built with raw lumber. I saw small windows with fabric tacked over the opening to keep out the mosquitos. Most men were boarded in a communal sleeping room, the sleeping spaces only separated by a curtain.

There were a few single rooms; my brother and I chose one of these. The room contained only a straw mattress, a blanket, a chamber pot, a desk with a chair, a basin of water and a bowl, and an extra mattress on the floor for Jamie. Food at the inn was simple: stew, bread, and coffee. It was good to get off the boat. After leaving Peru we may have rougher accommodations, but fewer companions, and everybody needs a bath.

Later, through the window we could hear the camp of the canal workers, and someone was playing a fiddle, an Irish melody I almost recognized, having heard some Irish music back in Detroit. Another canal worker accompanied on a soft low drum. After a while they gave it up and turned in, which benefited everybody.

As we traveled though the landscape westward, slowly eating up the miles, I thought: This country is changing rapidly. Between nearly unbroken forests you saw small settlements, temporary buildings, and young people flooding in, willing to live in privation while looking for an opportunity. Everyone seemed either to seek title to a piece of property, or some way bring in money by finding a trade or a merchant to attach themselves to, in order to make a new life.

Everywhere you saw increasing population, clearing, draining, and claiming the land; new building; settlers finding how to disengage the Indians' claims on the property, and to encourage them to leave. Soon the landscape will be very different.

The Last Indian Village In Indiana

We disembarked at the community of Peru on the south side of the Wabash River and found conveyance down the Mississinewa River to Mount Pleasant, where there was a Lenape and Miami Indian town and the Indian Chief Frances Godfroy had a trading post. We lodged in a cabin and bought food, until we connected with a trader traveling south to Indianapolis. It was an opportunity for us to rest, bathe, and wash our clothes, which required heating the water in great iron pots over a couple of days.

While Jamie talked privately with the Chief about the Underground Railroad through Detroit, I visited those village members who were willing. They were worried about rumors that they would be forced off this land. The Indians were intrigued by the opportunity to escape north, but pointed out they would have no community there. Black people who came north via the Railroad had already established small villages in Canada, but the American tribes, being different kinds of Indians with different cultures, had no places to go for the support of others. They would be adrift and alone. If they stayed with their own they would at least have community, even in a new place. Community and shared culture and understood roles are very important to them. And in Canada the experience of the native Indian tribes with the white settlers was no better than in America.

It was interesting to study the facial expressions of the Indians. They believe it is impolite in formal interactions to behave informally. Formal behavior demands an unmoving countenance and a direct gaze. This was only a little different from my own great-grandmother in my experience, and so I was able to interact and maintain the same aspect out of respect, although my features were more mobile by habit. I didn't realize before this that facial expressions are a cultural phenomenon, differing in different peoples.

One resident of the town, who I met but who did not want to talk, was a white woman who had lived with the Indians her whole life. She was called Maconaquah and was taken from Quakers in Pennsylvania as a very young girl by some tribespeople who had lost a daughter in conflict with the colonists. She had a large family there in the village and was devoted to her adopted culture. She was 67 years old.

The History of Anderson

After about a week at Mount Pleasant the trader arrived who would take us to Indianapolis. This man, Jimmy Bell was his name, transported goods, and sometimes passengers, between remote settlement markets and larger towns, and then returned with other goods to the trading post. We made our thanks to the Chief and settled up for the lodging and food, and set out on the next leg of the journey.

The trader's wagon was a buckboard, a single plank seat with a board back, wide enough for all three of us to sit on it, and a platform-type wagon behind. He had two horses, in order to pull three people, plus horse feed as well as his merchandise. He brought a little dog for safety during the nights. Other supplies included a rifle, a tent top for the wagon for the passengers to sleep under, a lean-to shelter and sleeping bag for the driver, and necessary food and clear water for each trip. This journey would take three days, as he needed to stop near the White River near Anderson. We waited for clear weather and brought enough provisions for two days of travel, planning to restock in Anderson area.

We followed the path of the Central Canal, which was surveyed but digging had only just begun. Because of all the work done to this point, there was a rough road along the planned canal path. You would call this kind of barely visible track a "trace". Its condition depended how many wagons had gone down it and how recently. Vegetation grew rapidly over the trace and you might have to "bushwhack" some new branches out of the way.

The wagon trace led down the Mississinewa, then left the river to cross overland through what is now Grant County and Madison County. At Anderson the canal trace picked up near the White River. Of course, canals follow topography, staying at low elevations and being filled with water from rivers. To climb a slope with a canal requires locks, which are a much bigger engineering project. The low-lying lands of the canals lend themselves to mosquitos, as we first experienced on the canal boat.

I marveled at how the trees changed as we went south from Michigan. The forest was overtaken by softwoods: ash, basswood, beech, maple. Far fewer of the dark green pine and broad oaks of our northern forests were seen. Instead the only evergreen is a native arborvitae, which grows rather large in the forest. Pretty, flowering shorter trees were mixed in with the leafed-out taller trees.

When we camped overnight, we pulled the wagon into a cleared spot alongside a stream. Trader Bell moved some trade goods aside, set up the canvas cover over the wagon bed, and arranged his own lean-to before boiling water for tea and soup. We sat around the fire with his little dog, and Jimmy Bell told us a story about the great "squirrel stampede" of 1822. Crop destruction was massive, and many squirrels died during this event. Bell said he thought the squirrels were reacting to trees being harvested for building materials, leaving less mast for the squirrels' food.

Overnight we had a little excitement when the dog heard noises in the woods and began madly barking. Jimmy Bell got up with a lantern and his rifle, but we stayed in the wagon. Jimmy decided it was just some deer and calmed the dog. We all went back to sleep until dawn, when we rose, repacked the wagon, and set out south again.

Anderson is a small town along the planned route of the Central Canal, which was to run along the White River to Indianapolis. While canal building was in its boom years, Anderson was incorporated and grew to a decent sized town; but after the crash of '37, when the state became bankrupt and paused much construction, the town shrank again.

Anderson Village was founded by Chief William Anderson, also known as Kikthawenund, a Lenape Indian Chief with a Swedish trader father. One of Chief Anderson's daughters, Mekinges, married William Conner, the founder of Noblesville, and bore him six children. It was politically expedient for Conner to have this high-status liaison with the native Indian tribes while establishing his trading and land business. In 1820 she and her children accompanied her community when they were removed to Kansas by treaty. Conner found it expedient to again marry within the year, this time to an 18-year-old well-connected white woman from his new town of Noblesville. Kikthawenund himself was removed to Kansas in 1830 with his people, his alliance with William Conner having benefited him not at all.

At Anderson we stayed overnight at a small inn – thank goodness! I ordered a bath. Jamie used it after me. We enjoyed the pause in travel while Trader Bell restocked. Our journey's last leg will be south, all the way to the east side of Indianapolis.

Conner House with Yellow Leaves by Sarah E. Morin

Slight Shadings by Ndaba Sibanda

degrees of dark and light
make a pic perfect or right,
if a peaceful poet poetises,

his voice vows, wows or even sensitises,
a poet's work is his potent yell or composition
through which he issues stars in a poetic fashion,
accustomed to free and fulfilling possibilities of human art,
his pen pours out shadings and meanings painted by his heart

Forgiveness by Donavan Barrier

I expected razor blades, knives, and fervent, furious condemnation
when you asked me to meet you that rainy day.
However, when I saw you, something emerged from you.
Butterfly kisses, a protective embrace, and white noise flowing from
your lips.
You whispered lovingly to me, six words that I did not deserve.
"I forgive you. It's all okay now."
I was ready for execution, but instead, I gained exoneration.
Before you took the key and unlocked my cell, I was a prisoner of my
own self-damnation.
I can now walk a free man because I received a pardon from you.
I can put the past behind me, thanks to you.

The Good Old Days by Vivianne Belle

my idea of the good old days
doesn't include racism or misogyny or Christian superiority
but rather it's simply childhood memories of
playgrounds and parks with other kids
a lot of whom didn't look like me
and I didn't care
at all

Suddenly Autumn Is Here by Jerry Dreesen

Pennies by John R Hinton

Sometimes to say hello to you
I have to say goodbye to me
Some people pass over the pennies on the ground
I stoop to pick them up
The old man in the grocery store
He's fallen to the floor
To say hello to him
I have to say goodbye to me
He needs my greeting to lift him
If I restrain my salutation
He has no worth in my eyes
Life the penny passed over by most
Valued only by a few
I stoop to pick him up
I say hello to him
I say goodbye to me
Collecting pennies, an act of grace
Not a grace given to others
An acceptance of grace for myself
I say hello to you
I say goodbye to me

Haiku-ing by Marilyn J Wolf

(a limerick about *haiku*)

Haiku are 5–7–5s.
Senryũ emotionally jives.
Both thoughtful to write,
they need to be tight
to move our husbands and wives.

Just a matter of History by JAC

Where you're born hits differently,
take into account that place;
did it disregard a certain race?
Does it often host a massive race?

How shells burst or muskets pow,
booming, then shrill, the still;
did it become so easy to forget freewill?
Does a land built on blood deserve more than an anthill?

What happened there wasn't perfect
fought over, feuded, or forfeited;
did a fire burn bright with creation or was it simply short-winded?
Does it often remind you to be reminded?

When a frozen giant came before you
and made waves you still surf,
absent of the awareness of pushed turf,
how many ascend this laudable *maulwurf*
only to forget history under a yellow dwarf?

Golden Autumn by Mairéad Lewis

27

Flightless Carrion by Rue Sparks

My darling, you were like a crow –
inky black eyes nestled in iridescent feathers
belying the mischief and intelligence that simmered beneath.
You held your trauma and pain close to your chest,
covered them with macabre humor and honeyed tales.
But I would know, because I did the same.

For you, I would become a corvid –
a twenty-year life span together like a honeymoon through a corn
maze.
We'd twist and dance through the dead ends and wrong turns,
laugh at our failures and hold hands as the night encroaches.

We spoke of our deaths as a distant thing –
a sudden crashing where our lives would end in each other's arms.
And if that was a dream, it was a kinder one;
crows mate for life, and maybe that's where we went wrong.

When the skies broke open,
and death clipped your wings,
we gathered like a cloak of shadows.
A murder of mourners that croaked our sorrows –
a crow funeral that lasted through the night.
But like a fog, lifted by the noonday sun.

I wished I could have given you a sky burial.
Let you watch the stars, and pick out shapes in the clouds
as you became one with the carrion birds.
Instead, I carry your ashes with me like Atlas,
knowing I can never let go of the things I lost and never said.

I leave trinkets and baubles by your shrine –
polished rocks, dandelions and colored shells.
And though I know you've given me all you had,
I ache that these gifts will never again be reciprocated.

There's no psychopomp, no Charon,
that can tear the remains of your soul from my chest,
or bring back the part of me that I buried with you.
And though the years pass,
like Poe, I still search for my Lenore.

In the scattered remembrance of my dreams in the morning light,
I hear the distance echo of the words, "Nevermore" –
and I can't tell if it was your voice or mine.

Nanstosuelta Flightless Carrion by Rue Sparks

Love Is . . . (variations in couplets) by Alys Caviness-Gober

I.

my arms, within my father's well-worn shirt,
holding this newborn baby, my grandchild

II.

enduring rock-hard agony of loss
weathering the blackened abyss of grief

III.

the look on a child's upturned face
discovering this world anew

IV.

the tingling moment of seeing your face
the brightness of being in the same place

V.

drifting to sleep beside you
as crickets sing in moonlight

Waterfront Views of Dreams: A Porter County Poem by Nancy Simmonds

Rafe and me worked the barges for years. More before the crash, o'course,
some workin' companies still needed lumber, railroad ties and ore.
We kept our heads down and our mouths shut and we worked steady enough
those lean years to keep food on the table and heat in the house. At least
most of the time. I 'member those years as gray 'cept for the blossoms on the trees
and the brown taters in the ground. Oh, and the white bellies of the fish
we snagged out of the Great Lakes.

Bright spots in those years? Not many, son, not many. But once't,
must a been about '35 or so, me and Rafe was asked to haul a house,

30

barge it from Chicago over to the dunes. It come from the Great Fair
and some feller was replanting it by his dream of a golf course
hoping it would somehow multiply. It was bright Almighty pink and
had a flat
roof that looked like some kind of ocean liner. The inside walls was
sunshine
yellow and blue bird blue and the color of a shell my ma kept on her
winder sill.
It sounds kinda silly but it sure were somethin'.

Rafe and me talked about it for a long, long time, what it would be like
to live in something like that. Plaster and clay tiles and aluminy-um
and all those big windows where people could see right inside you
like an aquarium or a flower garden or a dream.

Without a bit a trouble they got that thing planted up on a cliff at
Beverly Shores.
We'd see it if we had runs over to Michigan. Still there fars I know.
After the war me and Rafe took a road trip over to there. Like a lotta
dreams
that golf course never got built. That pink house didn't get any garden
colored companions. Just sits there in the weeds, paint peeling
windows shut to the gray lake. Asleep.

All Chains Are Equal by Mairéad Lewis 🌍

Dancing With a Stranger by Marilyn J Wolf

(view *On and On*: https://www.youtube.com/watch?v=ljuJnUYozUg)

Lunch break in the city.
Cars, cabs, trucks, people, noise everywhere.
Some with lunch,
some still to purchase.

Standing in line at the deli,
behind me a man
about my height
near my age, maybe.

On and On starts on the radio.
He and I sway to the music.
We smile at each other.
I say, "It's hard not to move when that's on."
He says, "I know."

He takes my hand
puts his arm around my waist
and we dance the rest of the song.

The other patrons applaud us.
We buy our lunches
and all have a better day
because of a song and a dance
in a deli.

A Lasting Burden by Chuck Kellum

The horror of war
Does not end.

Though it leaves the battlefield
With those who did not die,
It will not die

Until the very last

Of the ones who survive

Has from this world
Departed.

Is There Something UnAfrican? by Ndaba Sibanda

It is a country on the southernmost tip
of Africa, and it's a *proper name*
that has the word *Africa* in it.

Some of that Southern African nation's
official languages entail: Zulu, Sotho,
Ndebele, Xhosa, Venda, Tswana, and English.

This African nation is separated by the Limpopo River
from a landlocked country in Southern Africa whose political,
historical, cultural factors influence its linguistic landscape.

That both countries share historical, cultural, and linguistic
similarities is no debate, for instance, both citizens speak:
Sotho, Ndebele, Xhosa, Venda, Tswana, and English.

It is a country on the southernmost tip
of Africa, and it's a *proper name*
that has the word *Africa* in it.

What is *improper* is the lack of respect
for the sanctity of life; brutality and criminality
whether perpetrated by a citizen or an *immigrant.*

African leaders have a duty to serve the interests
of their nations and citizens in a total and true fashion,
anything else is inexcusable, unfit, and unacceptable.

What is also inexcusable, unfit, and unacceptable
is to slay another African citizen by virtue
of that he was an *undocumented immigrant.*

How sad that the words *Africa, African*
have lost their essence in a heartless pool

of Afrophobia, Xenophobia, or Anti-Africanism.

In both countries, one can find a Dube, a Khumalo,
a Mudau, a Ndlovu, a Nyathi, and even a Dlamini –
does their brotherhood diminish by virtue of borders?

How sad that artificial colonial boundaries have
overridden historical, cultural, and linguistic affinities
and humanity is haunted, blinded brothers like ghosts.

Indeed there is a race for wealth, jobs, power, and survival,
but what boggles me is that an undocumented non-black
African can live in there without hassles or eyebrows raised.

It is a country on the southernmost tip
of Africa, and it's a *proper name*
that has the word *Africa* in it.

Is there something *UnAfrican*?

Hole in the Air by Kenneth Conklin

They told me, time heals all.
 They said I should move on.
They told me she's in heaven,
 They said it was her time.
They said it was pre-ordained.
 They told me to find busy work
Find new friends, set new goals,
 Find a purpose.
They told me I'll get over her.
 I said, it's been a year,
And she's still not here.
 I still feel her spirit near,
Sitting in her easy chair,
 But it's not really her,
It's only a hole in the air.

34

Still Looking Good 2 by Jerry Dreesen

PICTURE OF MY GRANDMA

Strange
that people only know each other
locked in our parallel ages,
always 50 years apart, or 2.

Grandma quirks a brow
in the tape-laced photograph,
her lips about to open
and confide secrets
of who she is
in that precise moment.

In another dimension
I will climb trees with my mother,
claim senior breakfast discounts
with my great-niece,
and tape together
the complete picture
of loved ones' souls
through time.

– Sarah E. Morin

Picture of My Grandma by Sarah E. Morin

My Hands by Alys Caviness-Gober

From wrists to fingertips echo
my dad's age spots, my mother's cold caress
across my fever'd brow,
Grandmommy's elegance, Baba's spices,
Grandpa Al's callouses, and Dedo's imagination;
they are my hands.

36

Green Book: Huntington County by Nancy Simmonds

Brownie barks and I move from dream to summer night.
Through the open window I hear car doors slam
and laughter.
I slide quietly from between the sheets.
My sister stays asleep
as I tiptoe to the painted sill to lean against the screen.

Grandpa with a flashlight by the barn
chats with white shirted men in fancy shoes,
their faces dark and shiny in the glow of cigarettes.
The light points to the biffy house
then into the barn.
A lantern lit and bobbing now
up to the hay mow.
We've slept up there when all the cousins come
and the farmhouse overflows.
The hay tickles but it's thick and sweet.
The moon's a yardlight through the big mow door
open to the sky tonight alight with jazzing stars.
The moon's a spotlight on their welcome,
sleeping safe in this hay
unlike Whites Only beds in town.
The men make a place to rest
flapping the dust from the stack of old quilts
scaring the mice.
More laughter.

I watch Grandpa cross the yard.
Brownie turns circles and flops in the dust by the barn door.
I slip back in bed next to my sister.
I hear the back screen clap shut
the creak on the stairs
Grandma saying something
and Grandpa's reply.
I fall asleep to a harmonica lullaby.

Tomorrow there will be biscuits and bacon, goat cheese
wrapped in waxed paper and tied with string on the kitchen counter.

After morning chores in the garden
the bar soap by the well pump will be wet
the old car will be gone
and there might be
some silver coins in the flower pot
by the back screen door.

Hiraeth for the Holidays by Jeff Couch

It was the beat that woke the man up. Not that it took much to wake him these days; he tossed and turned most nights and never felt like he actually got any sleep. He thought about opening his eyes, but didn't want to use the effort it would take. He focused instead on what his ears were hearing. Nothing. He started to fade back asleep.

There it was again. That incessant beat. *Boom, boom, boom*. He reached over to see if Amanda was awake. His hand fell onto the cold sheets of the empty bed next to him. Right, Amanda wasn't there. He hated when he forgot. His eyes felt like someone was carving them out with a spoon as the tears began to well up again. He wouldn't be sleeping for a little while but he lay there trying. It was no good. Frustrated, he wiped his cheeks dry and opened his eyes.

This time he was waiting for it when it came. *Boom, boom, boom*. Flat on the bed, he couldn't tell where it was coming from; might as well sit up. The cold air raked its fingertips across his bare shoulders as the blanket fell to the mattress. He sat on the edge of the bed waiting. He was way too old to be afraid of the dark, but the empty blackness still spooked him. He felt like one of his prehistoric ancestors waiting for the predator in the darkness. He sat there trying to ignore the feeling that there was something creeping up from behind.

This time he could tell it came from out front, just the other side of the wall. He grabbed some slippers and a shirt. He didn't bother to button it; he would just be a moment, he just had to see what that noise was. He paused at the door, wishing he had gotten around to installing the peephole. Amanda had asked him to, a million times; so many things he'd meant to do. So many things he'd meant to say. There'd been so much time . . . and then there wasn't any more. He pressed his head against the cold metal of the door and took a breath to steady himself.

No more tears. Not tonight. Just a few hours. Just a little break. No more tears. Please?

With his head against the door, he could hear more; it sounded like children singing. What were they singing? It sounded vaguely familiar. Then it came again. *Boom, boom, boom.* He knew he'd heard it before, but the melody was just out of reach. Quietly, so as not to startle the children, he opened the door.

The night was quiet, bright, and crystal clear. The moon shone radiant and nearly full. The stars were intense and sharp. It was as if someone carved the night out of a block of black ice. He stood on his lawn looking up at the stars when he heard it again. This time the high-pitched voices rang out sweetly in the crisp air.

Veinticinco de diciembre, fum, fum, fum,
Veinticinco de diciembre, fum, fum, fum.

It wasn't *boom, boom, boom*, it was *fum, fum, fum*. That was it; the creepiest of all Christmas carols. He hadn't heard it for years – probably not since his teens. He remembered now. He remembered the radio, with all the strange music. No "Frosty the Snowman" or "Rudolph the Red-Nosed Reindeer." No, their songs, their… "villancicos" – that's what they were called, all hundreds of years old. Not marketing schemes by a downtown department store; no, these songs had been birthed in an ancient monastery somewhere by somber monks trying to instill the fear of God in the village children. They seemed so strange and ominous when he was little; now they just reminded him of home. A home he hadn't lived in for 30 years.

Where was it coming from? He stepped off the sidewalk and started to walk down the middle of the street.

A la tierra rutilante que relumbra con su luz,
Y a la paz del firmamento celebrando el Nacimiento, fum, fum, fum.

He couldn't see anything, but the children had to be right here – the song was so clear.

Veinticinco de diciembre, fum, fum, fum.
Veinticinco de diciembre, fum, fum, fum.

With every *fum* his heart leapt into his throat and bumped against the knot lodged there. That knot had been stuck in his larynx for months.

He didn't know if it would ever go away. He wandered down the black road in the black night, looking down every side street. How could there be children caroling ancient Spanish Christmas songs in the middle of an American Midwestern city in the middle of the night? He was so confused. He half-expected Amanda to shake him awake and tell him he was only dreaming.

Venid con la pandereta y castañuelas al portal,
a adorar al rey del cielo que ha aparecido en el suelo, fum, fum, fum.

So many Christmas memories were flooding back. The hard crunch of *turrón* from Alicante, the soft sweetness of the one called Jijona. And the *polvorones*, the powdery dry cookies that melted in your mouth. Whenever he had tried to describe them, no one ever grasped how they tasted so good; his descriptions never made them sound like the dreamy delights they were. Amanda hadn't really understood either, but that hadn't stopped her from going online one year and ordering all of them, boxes and boxes of them, as a special Christmas surprise. He'd come home from work and there they all were, stacked up on the table. She was standing beside the pile, beaming. It had taken a month to eat it all.

He gasped and bent over at the waist; that memory had hurt. Why did the good memories hurt so much more? He tried to straighten up, but there was a cramp in his chest. He looked down and saw what looked like a giant shriveled-up fruit sticking out of his chest. It was dark and leathery and looked like it'd been left to rot. It was big, though. He wasn't sure how he could stand upright with this giant, rotted mass hanging down his left side with his shirt flapping against it. He looked at it. That's when it opened its eyes and looked back at him.

"*¡Oye tío!* How's it hangin'? Oh, I guess **I am.** *¡Ja, ja, ja, ja!*" It laughed a raspy, hacking cough. Dumbfounded, he realized that it wasn't a fruit hanging there, but rather something like a gargoyle with its arm buried in his chest. He just stood there and stared at the thing. This night was very strange. Very strange indeed.

"Um, hi. Who are you?" It wasn't clever, but it was all he could think of to say.

The creature opened its mouth to speak. The thing was a foot from his face and the voice coming out was harsh and raspy. It sounded like its lungs were on fire from some terminal disease.

40

"*¡I'm El Duende, tío! ¡And* you…are not! *¡Ja, ja, ja, ja!*" It started its hacking, burning laugh again.

"Um, could you get off me please? This is kind of uncomfortable."

"No way, *tío*! That's what I am here for. It is supposed to be uncomfortable. No, I'm not leaving at all."

With that, the little creature twisted its arm, the arm piercing the man's chest. He realized now that the creature had a hold of his heart. He gasped with pain as the little monster squeezed it.

"Get off me now!" He tried to push it off.

"*¡Uh, uh, uh!*" The creature squeezed his heart again; this time, the squeeze came with a memory.

He was in the back of a large group of teenagers. He was excited because this was the first year he had been invited to come along. It was midnight and they were standing outside the house of some important family. They were all trying to be quiet, but there was so much giggling and pushing and good-natured jockeying for position that they were failing terribly at being surreptitious. The brave one in the front rang the doorbell and they waited for someone to appear. The door opened, and they all burst into song. It was the worst version of *We Wish You a Merry Christmas* he'd ever heard. They were all more concerned with volume than value. After a verse in Spanish, they all switched to English. The accents were awful, but nobody cared. They were all having a good time. For once he felt like he was a part of the group, like he really belonged. He wished he could stay connected like this forever.

The memory faded, and the pain hit him hard. He gasped as his heart ached where the little demon grasped it in its hand.

"Now you see, *tío*. And remember, there is more where that came from. You play nice with me and maybe I go easy on you. Then again…*¡Ja, ja, ja, ja!*" Sandpaper on a chalkboard. That was what its laugh sounded like. Or something equally as awful. The man was starting to hate that sound. He stumbled forward. Maybe if he could just keep moving, the thing would fall off. All thoughts of the children's choir were gone. Just keep moving. One step, two steps, three steps. The night had turned silent. He looked down and the imp smiled up at him with a fiendish smile. Oh, no! It twisted its arm and squeezed. Another memory.

He was supposed to be watching for Santa, but instead he was in a room packed with people. He barely knew these grown-ups and they were all speaking quickly, so fast he couldn't understand them. They were all very loud and there was a lot of laughing. He thought they were acting a little strange and it probably had something to do with the weird-smelling liquid in their glasses. They had offered him a sip and he'd spat it out; it was gross. That just made them laugh harder.

He looked and saw that there were platters of cheese and meat and bread placed all over the room, and a box of individually wrapped cookies. He glanced around to see if anyone was looking and then grabbed one. It said *Roscón de vino* on the plastic. He had no idea what that meant but it looked like a little powdered donut. He loved those, and he hadn't seen one since they moved here. He carefully tore the plastic off and bit into it. To his surprise it wasn't soft and fluffy; it was hard and crunchy. At first he didn't like it, but then he realized it was delicious! He quickly grabbed another one before someone told him to stop. It was way past his bedtime, and he figured he'd better eat as many as he could before someone realized he was still up and sent him away. Maybe this was better than waiting up for Santa.

The man let out a yell. "Ahhhh!" He didn't mean to say anything, but that memory had really hurt. "Mr. Duende sir, do you think you could stop with the twisting my heart thing?"

"*¡Ay no! ¿*What is wrong with you, *tío*? First of all, it is **EL** Duende, not mister. Second of all, you are lucky. You get a visit from me. *¡Felicidades!* I'm not going away for a while. You see, tonight is the solstice, *el solsticio*, the longest night of the year. It is MY night, *mi noche eterna. ¡*You are mine tonight, *tío! ¡Ja, ja, ja, ja!*" It laughed like a wool afghan on a sunburn, the kind you get after playing all day at the beach in the tropical sun with no lotion because none of your friends needed any, but your skin was always as pale as *leche frita* – fried milk – or at least that is how a cute girl put it. Yeah, that was what its laugh was like.

The man continued wandering down the street. He was in a daze, barely able to tell where he was or when. The physical ache in his heart matched the emotional one. The night stretched out before him, dark and endless. He didn't even notice when the beast twitched again; memory.

Christmastime was finally here! Mommy had said he could order anything he had wanted off the menu. He had asked for hot chocolate, but this . . . this was nothing like any hot chocolate he'd ever had. It was so thick he could almost stand up his spoon in it! On his plate was a loop of warm cinnamony pastry. It was crisp on the outside and light and airy on the inside. He broke off a piece and dipped it in the chocolate like the waiter said to: the chocolate clung to the pastry and melted in his mouth into a rich, dark, sweet . . . his young mind ran out of words. It was amazing and like nothing he had ever tasted. He didn't know how to describe it; all he knew is that he wanted more. He quickly broke off another piece and plunged it into his mug. Christmas in this country was delicious!

Now the man could taste that memory. When was the last time he'd had chocolate *con churros*? He remembered the time Amanda tried to make some for him. She had failed so miserably. The chocolate was gluey and clumpy, and the *churros* were hard and dense like scones. She had been so upset. She hadn't really understood how much it had meant to him that she'd wanted to give him a little of what he was missing. And now she was missing, too.

He was starting to have trouble breathing. The ache had crept up into his lungs. He wasn't sure how much more of this he could take. He looked down at the misshapen thing crouched above his belly. Its rheumy yellow eyes looked at him, unblinking. "Please, no more. *El Duende*, sir, I beg of you. Please! I don't think I can take any more!"

"*¡Tonterías!* You speak such foolishness. I know you have the capacity for so much more suffering. I am sure of it, *tío*. I don't even know why you are so upset. Those memories you are having, they don't even belong to you. Those are from *otro país*, that is not your *cultura*. You are a *Yanqui, tío*. You have no right to miss those things. *No te pertenecen, tío*. They don't belong to you. *¡Ja, ja, ja, ja!*"

Ay, mi madre! He hated that laugh! Hated it! Worse: the fiend was right. He wasn't Spanish, he was born in America and, except for a few years, had lived there for most of his life. At best his ancestry was . . . Welsh maybe? How could he claim these memories? They were not his cultural birthright. Then it came. Another twitch, another twist.

They were all inside, while he stood on the balcony watching them. All his friends; the family he'd made. They were laughing and having fun with the Christmas gift exchange. It was always so sweet; everyone handmade their gifts and tailored them to each recipient. No one had much money or, if they did, they pretended not to, so that no one would feel left out or insufficient. Some gifts were sentimental, some were funny, but they were all heartfelt. That was real love in there. That was a family of friends. That was the sound of home.

Tomorrow he would get on a plane. Tomorrow he would leave. Who knew if he would ever come back? He wanted to stay, but he wasn't old enough to make that decision, was he? Besides, no one understood the problem; he was going home, wasn't he? He was going to where his family was, to where his heritage was, his country. He would make new friends. He would forget this place and be happy back where he belonged. He was just being immature. He was nearly grown now, he needed to act that way. If that was so, then why did he feel like he was leaving behind everything he cared about? Why did it feel like he was leaving home and going to a foreign land? He looked out over the edge of the iron railing one last time and tried to cement the view in his mind. He would never forget what home looked like.

The man realized he'd thought he would never find home again; he would never have that kind of family. But then he had found Amanda. They had built a family, just the two of them. He had forgotten the pain of leaving it all behind. Forgotten it, until last year, December 29th. Another twist, and with it, another memory.

He was looking down at Amanda, lying in a hospital bed. It made no sense. She was the one that had so much to offer the world. She was the one with the loving smile. She was the one that cared and loved and gave until there was nothing left. He was the selfish one. She was the one that made the world a better place. Without her, who would remind the sun to rise in the morning and the birds to sing?

This was a mistake. He needed to let someone know that they were making a mistake. Someone in charge who could fix things. But there was no one who could fix this. As he sat there by her side, people came and went. They said, "Be happy," and, "She is going to a better place; she is going home." They didn't understand. She **was** home. She was **his** home. Without her, where would he go? Without her, where was home? This was all wrong. Nothing about this was right. He reached over and brushed away the hair from her face. He took another look at her, so he could remember what home looked like.

The man stumbled. He had reached a flight of stairs in the middle of the city; if this was in Europe, it would be in the central plaza. But this was not Europe; it the middle of America, and this was some monument in the middle of a traffic circle in the middle of the city in the middle of the night.

He kept walking forward, falling up the steps until he collapsed at the top. He bent over, gasping for air. The pain was in his whole body now. It radiated out from his chest and every muscle ached. He could no longer tell what was emotional, what was physical, what was present, what was past. Every part of him hurt. Every breath hurt, every pause between breaths hurt, his open eyes hurt, his closed eyes hurt, his throat hurt, and his heart hurt, and it all rose up in him until he opened his mouth and out came the sound of a man drowning in sorrow.

"Aiiiiiiiiiiiiiiiii!" One long note, held for longer than breath could be. Again.

"Aiiiiiiiiiiiiiiiiiii!" It rang out in the clear air. The ache shifted to his belly, his diaphragm. It now needed words.

No te vayas de mi lado Don't leave my side
No puedo vivir sin verte I can't live without seeing you.

To his right a ghostly figure of a man appeared, was dressed in a white, blousy shirt and straight black pants. He held a guitar that he struck like a drum as often as he strummed it.

Sin oír tu dulce canto Without hearing your sweet song
Sin sentir tu dulce amor Without feeling your sweet love.

To his left appeared a ghostly lady, her hair pulled back into a slick tight bun, wearing a tight red dress covered in large black polka dots that flared at the bottom into a long train. She danced a fluid, stomping, elegant dance. Her feet hit the ground in dramatic rhythms with her body rigidly upright as her arms formed precise angles and shapes. One hand held the train of her dress; she moved as if it were part of her body, dancing along with her.

No te vayas de mi vida Don't leave my life
No puedo seguir sin tenerte I can't go on without having you.

Five men in blousy shirts and straight black pants with flat-brimmed hats appeared. They began dancing with the same stomping pattern, their hands also raised at right angles, clapping in time to the beat of the guitar and the stomping of the feet. The music rose to a fever pitch.

No te vayas de mi lado Don't leave my side
No te vayas de mi Don't leave me
No te vayas de mi Don't leave me.
No te vayas de mi…

With that, it felt like he had squeezed every ounce of anguish from his soul. He had pushed it and carved it out of his body. The dancing continued as the guitar played on. Then, as the music ebbed, the dancers and musicians slowly faded away. The man looked down. *El Duende* was still there. It smiled. Nothing about its appearance changed, but the shriveled little thing with the oversized nose and haunting eyes looked strangely kind and gentle. As sunlight began to creep over the edge of the buildings, the little goblin gave one last twist of its arm, smiled its strangely sweet smile and, just like the music, faded away.

The man sat with tears streaming down his face and watched the sunrise. He didn't know how he was going to make it through tomorrow, but he knew that he would. He had done it before, and he knew he would do it again. He would miss a home that could never be found again, but he'd find a new home. It wouldn't be a substitute for the old one. The ache would always be there, and when it got too bad, *El Duende* would come and squeeze his heart until he cried out his pain. And then, somehow, it would be better for a while. Somehow, he would take one step, and then another.

He stood up and began to walk back to his house. Maybe he should invite some people over for Christmas brunch. There were still a couple of days left before the holiday. Or maybe he could find a charity that needed new volunteers. He wasn't sure what he was going to do, but he knew it was time. It was time, once again, to start building a new home.

Autopsy of Prometheus by Rue Sparks

Pain is my constant companion –
It settled like a blanket over my skeleton.
With it, the slow dissipation of tomorrows and some days,
and the birth of the bucket list and calls about accessibility.

As the years pass by,
still no closer to a cure or comfort,
my time is filled with diagnostics and prescriptions.
The faces of nurses and specialists become a dissonant blur,
coalescing into a visage of a stoic Victor Frankenstein
hovering next to my bedside.

His static humming, inane chatter
of statistics and improbabilities,
blame and dismissals,
reveal his silent judgment.

As he saws into my rib cage to get to my heart,
I want to tell him – he's looking at the wrong muscle.
It's an ache in my bones,
a burning in my lungs,
a bursting, boiling thrumming in my brain
that keeps me up at night

But he's no longer listening.
His ears filled with the cotton of his ideologies,
and my voice is drowned out
by unrepentant platitudes and distracted disregard,
as he dissects each valve and chamber.

I become an amalgamation of his theories and accusations,
sutured together with steel wire and metal plates.
And if I am no longer something human,
I am led to believe that it is my fault
for finding myself on his surgical table.

And maybe it's fitting, I think,
that Frankenstein's creation is never given a name.

Because to see his creation as anything but imperfect and inhuman,
he'd have to reconcile the heart he had dissected,
the soul he had mangled.
In that trying to heal, he had vandalized.
Because when it counted, he was too proud to be human,
and chose to be the monster he always feared he'd create.

Addiction by Jerry Dreesen

An addiction – cable news.
I am determined
not to watch
this morning. It would be
the same
"Breaking News" – the same
disturbing videos, shocking
descriptions of events
I heard yesterday. Still –
What if I don't watch?
What if something really
important happened
and I missed it?
Just be patient I tell myself.
It'll be on Twitter or on a
Late Show monologue.
But still –
I need to turn it on.
"Breaking News"
It might really be important
this time.

a cacophony of crows
unable or unwilling
to reach a compromise

Why Poetry Polishes And Procures by Ndaba Sibanda

I use the power of poetry to describe
what smells, because its sense of smell
is trustworthy and authoritative like a king.

The bear, shark, snake, dog, kiwi, cow, moth,
rat, horse are the animals with the best sense
of smell, but poetry perfectly leads the pack.

Be it a strong sense of family, a sense of sight,
a sense of direction, humor, poetry is spot on,
hence I use its power to direct or humor humans!

I use the power of poetry to describe
a variety of sounds because its hearing knack
is the envy of my ears, poetry has pure earholes!

I see the world through the lens of poetry
because poetry inspects without winking
better than a microscope, binoculars, or goggles.

Poetry knows how to punch words into perfection,
passionate pastors use poetry for their sermons,
I think felons use words as beacons to decoy.

Poetry knows how to punch words into perfection,
marvelous musicians use poetry to mesmerize,
all lovely lovers speak the language of poetry well.

Poetry is romantic, it knows when to touch
and where to touch and how to touch and wow!
it knows all the textures, tastes, emotions, and shapes.

The Waters of Lethe by Dorothy Lorant

I do not fear *nightmares* for they are the stuff of transient terror … a
faceless wraith, a looming menace, a dark street where shadows lurk.

These are mere painted devils easily dismissed, knowing they come in
error having chosen my nocturnal address by mistake.

They have no power to linger when I wake, dissolving quickly into
mist, spilling neither anguish on the coming day, nor a sense of dread.

49

They are the stuff of children's fairy tales, and if for an instant they persist … the ogre in the closet, the monster under the bed … their specter is soon shed.

It is *dreams* that leave me inconsolable, for dreams have the power to kill, reanimating memories buried in a shallow grave, patient and still, waiting to ambush the unsuspecting heart and shatter a fragile serenity carefully forged, a bulwark I once thought unbreachable in its tenacity.

Locked in the fastness of sleep, Dream … *a malignant incubus who fattens on grief* … delivers a snatch of song, a face, an echo of laughter, that lulls me for a brief radiant moment before snatching the illusion away, leaving me stricken anew, and I am undone by sadness that lacerates my heart and takes me to a place where dreams kill, love happened only once, and the waters of Lethe never flow.

Dreams have your measure … the height of your love, the depth of your sorrow The length of years spent insulating self from a loss beyond tears. Dreams keep a record, like an insect in amber, of moments in Time filled with laughter, joy, the certainty of love, until the day you drifted down the air never once looking back o'er a chasm of years.

And when I am undone, Dream whispers in my ear, "I can kill you softly with memories that make every breath a sob. Or swiftly, if it pleases me, to rob you of tranquility. And just when you think to die of sorrow and regret, I will leave … until you are lulled into believing I forget."

"Why do you hate me so?" I ask.
"Because you are a fool," Dream sneers, "Before, I was constrained by Time and Space, but now, by putting words to pen, you give me form and face. And we two will walk hand-in-hand 'til there remains of you no trace. You call me 'Dream' but my name is 'You.' And not even the Waters of Lethe will give you peace.

    And you shall fear me more when I'm away
    Not knowing my return … the hour, the day."

Looking Out of a Covered Bridge by Sarah E. Morin

Women March Onward by Alys Caviness-Gober

She tripped at first, footing unsure,
balance precarious;
her steps faltered, arms outstretched
trying to steady herself
as she moved slowly forward;
her legs ached at first,
muscles unused to movement
cried out at the injustice,
pulsing in agony and anger
at her forcing them against their will;
she kept on moving, progressing,
advancing, evolving, taking
one step at a time until
her muscles were fluid and her steps sure;
yet the horizon, as always,
remained a faraway dream.

Poppy by Alison Harlos

I gasp with this first girl
I watch as each new pod unfurls
Her slow dance
Reminds to pause.
One by one, grace and color, unmatched
7 days

On Loss by Kenneth Conklin

Old, alone, and sad.
Replied the old man.
To the young woman.
At the grief seminar.
Can you say more?
She inquired.
Yes, said he, I can.
My wife passed way
She was my soulmate
And other half.
Then our church closed,
And those friends
Went elsewhere.
Other friends quit
Calling and
Seemed to disappear
Leaving me with
a broken heart
an empty home
And her photo
On the wall.
So, here I sit
Old,
alone, and sad.

Bursts of Pink by Marilyn J Wolf

Rockers croak over pavers
sitting in the early morning.
Breeze blows through the screen
through me.
Trees and leaves rustle.
Pool waterfall sheds prisms.
Ice-colored ripples at that end.

I hear the sunrise.
Pale blue sky thrums,
morning edges rhythmic,
fluffy clouds beating pink.

A white ibis flies.
Gently curved bill
slender head neck
feet following
wings stroke slowly.

Breeze stops
water turns to glass
as the ibis nears.
It flies directly over the pool.
I taste the air from wing strokes.

Pink sunrise embraces
head, neck, belly, wings, legs.

A perfect pink ibis in the air and on the pool.
I feel the shimmer
between
as they become One in those seconds.
My breath catches.

(Untitled senryū) by Chuck Kellum

We are given names
George?, Frank?, Emily?, Susan? . . .
And they become us

Coventry, England, November 14-15, 1940, Before The Resurrection
by Bonita Cox Searle 🌍

and after the Luftwaffe bombers
severed Coventry's arteries of
water and gas,
electricity and phone,

after they
cratered the roads
where the ambulances
and fire wagons stumbled
to save the unsavable,

after the medieval city of
Lady Godiva disappeared in
miles long, miles high
smoke and fire
that hid the clear night sky
with its glorious Mourning Moon
and hid the mangled bodies of those
who never asked for war,

after the Cathedral of St. Michael
caught fire and screamed louder than the
incessant wailing of air raid sirens,
its tremendous nails
flung through the air as if
the Warrior Saint were battling
the Devil Himself,

after the sirens stopped
and the fire winds ceased,
two beams,
smoldering and charred,
came to rest
in the form
of a cross
almost
too heavy to bear.

April 6ᵗʰ by Jerry Dreesen

Origins by Mona Mehas 🌍

Editors' note: it is sometimes hard to strike a balance between respecting artistic freedom and recognizing current terminology when referring to the history of marginalized groups. Whether fiction or based on historical fact, we have chosen to let some language stand, even when terminology has been updated in popular culture to respect cultural norms.

The Diaspora of Gypsies was the name of a poster on my classroom wall. It was decorated with arrows and maps and women in fancy skirts. I read that Gypsies were taken as slaves in the eighth century from India to Northern Africa, supposedly by the dreaded Turks; others sold themselves into the military. Wherever they landed, and for whatever reason, they had children with those already there. Europeans believed they all came from Egypt, and some did, so they were called Gypsies. My ancestors made their way from Egypt into Europe, thinning their gene pool as they traveled, but their music and stories remained rich. In my soul, I'm a wanderer. My mother's family had olive skin and dark hair. My blonde hair and blue eyes came from the one who fathered me.

Don't Race by Ndaba Sibanda

My poem is an opposite, reverse, backward one,
a yellow sky, the sum of none but red and green,
my poem is prose like a piece of icy rays in the sun,
I've tried my hand at an epic, acrostic, not this one,
I, who penned an autobiography which isn't mine!

I've tried my hand at haiku, bio, but not this one,
It's like free verse which is unliberated, this one!
All those poetic forms filled me with a ton of fun,
this one is as sweet as tucking into some lemon,
what happens when life throws a misplaced pun
at you? Stun it, turn it into a bun, that's dad's opinion,
when life frowns into a hell, smile into your heaven,
son, anyone, any human has an option, it's open,
run at your pace, don't race, that's the mission!

No One Else by Chuck Kellum
for Julie

You love me like no one else
In all the things you do.
Ever, always, the only one
Whose love has been most true.

Companion, lover,
Playmate, friend, . . .
Sharing freely
Time
   and again,
And with me always
To the end.

• ♥ •

You give to me your fullest self.
You love me
Like no one else.

Life's brought us much and sometimes little;
Sometimes we're strong and sometimes brittle;
Sometimes we're low and sometimes high;
Sometimes we laugh and sometimes cry.

And though your charms have captured me,
Within your arms I've been set free.

I give to you my fullest self.
I love you
Like no one
else.

First Kiss by Alys Caviness-Gober

she never really understood
the boy-crazy girls
in junior high and high school
and an older boy scared her
when he told everyone
he wanted to be her first kiss

– even then that seemed creepy –

it took a while through her
from-afar crushes on a few boys
for her to even contemplate a kiss
and when she imagined a kiss
she couldn't help but think
saliva swapping seemed gross

– she already knew fairy tales don't come true –

cool night air descended
October leaves scratched above
as they stood in her treehouse
and she could see the kitchen window
and her mother moving
back and forth across its light

– without warning he leaned down and kissed her –

startled she stepped back
he said *it's my braces isn't it*
you don't like me
his beautiful eyes bespoke the youthful pain
and awkwardness of self-consciousness
and poignant need for assurance

she leaned towards him and
whispered *yes I do*
and kissed him back

– the old woman sighs remembering –

the reality rather than wishful revision of her history
when suffused in the paralysis of naiveté
she had not said a word

The Suicide by Dorothy Lorant

(For KP, died March 10, 2022)

In barely a fortnight, two weeks at best, you will settle in your favorite chair, ostensibly to rest. But still a final task awaits, the journey to a better place than you inhabit now. A place you have no concept of, you say … perhaps the vast uncharted corridors of space, to spend a quiet eternity without deformity and pain.

And so, with steady hand, you will affix a mask, breathe deeply of the noxious gas you bought to be delivered from an unrelenting foe.

A kind and gentle man, he seeks no favors of Life; indeed feels himself well-served these 60 years surrounded by the things he loves most … the dogs he has rescued from abuse, his books and music.

His is a droll sense of humor, enabling him to look at the world's insanity without despair, certain that man's essential goodness will always eventually prevail.

But what paralyzes him with dread is a vile and ugly life without vision or voice, the inability to swallow, and soon, without choice … for even now the invading tentacles of an insatiable killer are probing his brain seeking entry.

And all that medicine can offer is a feeding tube, an artificial voice box, a white cane, and the prospect of a month or two trapped in a body that is closing down every option until all that remains is an empty husk.

"Are you disappointed in me?" he asks, knowing that for me, to take one's own life is the ultimate abandonment of God. But I cannot, will not, speak words of reproof or rebuke. Nor do I try to dissuade him.

And so I say, "I have no vote, my dear, no say in this … for yours is a path I am not walking, and who am I to stay the hand that brings release if that is your wish."

I will not threaten, as did the friend who screamed in anger, "I can stop you, you know! Alert the police, have you committed somewhere you will be restrained from self-harm and danger."

Yes, I scorn. And when you have stripped him of comfort and peace, because *you* cannot cope with the ugly grimness of his affliction, you will return home, three states away, unctuous, complacent, feeling more fastidious than God.

And when word reaches you that he has died by his own hand, you will rail against him, denounce his choice … but from afar, of course, your never having returned or called or spoken a word of comfort or farewell. When speaking of him, you will feign sadness, ruing to all who will listen of his inevitable banishment in hell.

An atheist, my friend has no such fear of waking from suicide into eternal damnation. Nor do I. For the God I believe in does not exact vengeance, mercy denied. And yet … what if I am wrong?

An old Spanish proverb has a hard, relentless God warning, "Choose what you will. Then pay for it."

"What will you choose?" God queries. "Sentiment versus my divine law? Pity versus piety? Love thy neighbor versus Thou shalt not kill?"

And so I look inside and ponder, "Is this a test also of me? Will I, undone by pity, deny my own belief that life is sacred?" Already I suffer guilt for failing to speak a single word to move him from his chosen course. And has my silence been construed as consent by an implacable, inflexible God?

And when, most often in the night, I lay stricken with sadness, my plight the fear of losing both a friend and my own immortal soul … when most bowed down and weary with unrest, I hear a voice echo in the canyons of my mind:

"Dear foolish child, think thee that *you* can ever be as loving, understanding, tender-hearted as Me? Or that I have but *one yardstick* by which I measure the human heart? It is I and I alone who have known him, by name, since the beginning of Time. And if he comes to my house a few days sooner by a trace, think thee I will slam the gates of Heaven in his face? Ah dearest child, dost thou not know that I am foolishly fond of my children, especially the suffering and the frail? And when I take a hand in Mine dost thou not know what it entail? That none can wrest that child from my embrace."

And thus wrapped in peace, I sleep.

All Dressed Up by Mairéad Lewis 🌍

60

The Mother of Rock and Roll by Dr. Leah Leach

"But I can do math!" I shouted.

I never thought that a fight with my husband over who invented rock and roll would contain that phrase, but it did.

I was born the same year The King, Elvis Presley, died. I was an impressionable kid when The King of Pop, Michael Jackson, was at the top of the charts. I sang the Queen of Soul, Aretha Franklin, hits when I was pregnant with my daughter. I grew up thinking rock and roll began with Bill Haley & His Comets' *Rock Around the Clock* (1954).

I was wrong.

It wasn't until I started the Gal's Guide Library, the first women's history lending library in the country, that I learned rock and roll was invented by a bi-sexual black woman. Her name was Sister Rosetta Tharpe, and the world, at one point, forgot about her. There are LOTS of thick books and some lengthy documentaries out there about the history of rock and roll. There is also a lot of debate in music history; we still can't agree on who invented the electric guitar. To give some context, here's my recap on what are the agreed-upon roots of rock and roll.

Rock and roll started in America as rhythm and blues in the Black communities in the 1930s. It wasn't called rock and roll or rhythm and blues in the '30s; it was called race music, and sometimes it was called sepia or Harlem hit parade. Just like segregation at water fountains, there was the separation of chart records, like Billboard, for music featuring Black artists. The music was a mix of gospel spirituals from church, work songs from the cotton fields, and sprinkled in was a dose of big band and jazz.

After World War II ended in 1945, prosperity in white middle class America boomed. White teenagers had more free time and spending money, and they were not amused by radio's wholesome sounds of Perry Como and Frank Sinatra. They looked to other stations on the dial – they found rhythm and blues stations. When Ohio radio DJ Alan Freed got wind of what white teenagers were listening to, he started playing rhythm and blues on his mainstream station. In 1951, he started calling it "rock and roll" and sales of race records saw huge increases. Record producers for white recording artists took notice and wanted in;

covers were made of white performers singing hits recorded by Black artists, and unfortunately, the covers outsold the originals.

Around this time, Sam Phillips was in Memphis recording Black rhythm and blues artists, thinking that the real money was in finding a white guy who could sing like them – he found Elvis Presley.

Elvis and his friend George Klein spent Sundays going to Black churches and listening to gospel; in a cultural reversal, George Klein later talked about how they had to sit in the back. Gospel was a major influence on Elvis' singing and style. And do you know of whom he was a big fan, whose records he would try to emulate? The number one gospel singer in the world – Sister Rosetta Tharpe.

When Elvis walked into Sun Studios, Marion Kessler asked him who he sounded like. Elvis famously said, "I don't sound like nobody." Well, when Sister Rosetta Tharpe was compared to male guitar players she'd say, "Can't no man play like me. I play better than a man." Elvis got a lot of his bravado from seeing Sister Rosetta perform; she was doing her thing since Elvis was in diapers, but, "That's all right now mamma."

With America's white DJs, record producers, and artists co-opting this style and targeting white teenagers, they were white-washing the originators. Still, white teens sought out the originals and because of that, mainstream radio stations started playing Chuck Berry, Fats Domino, Little Richard, and more. Many historians like to say the first rock and roll song was *Rocket 88* by Ike Turner, released in 1951. Ike Turner claimed a lot of things, so facts help. There were songs before *Rocket 88* that had the same feel, like Fats Domino's *The Fat Man* (1950), but you need to look further back than the '50s, something rock and roll historians are not apt to do.

In 1938, Sister Rosetta released a single, *That's All*. The song featured an upbeat electric guitar rhythm, amazing pickin', and a guitar solo. Gospel in lyrics, gospel in musical styling, not quite jazz, not quite swing, not quite blues, hm . . . what to call it? The following year she released the album *The Lonesome Road* which contained *Rock Me* and *This Train*.

In 1942 Maurie Orodenker, a music reviewer for Billboard, described Sister Rosetta's vocals as, "Rock-and-roll spiritual singing." It's said to be the first time the phrase "rock-and-roll" was used in print. Keep in mind this is nine years before Alan Freed is credited with coining the term "rock and roll."

"But I can do math!" I shouted.

I love music, but there are serious blind spots when it comes to the math. The legend of Ike Turner making the first rock and roll record shouldn't be as ironclad as it is when you have a record from 1938 that has the same elements. The Ohio thing really gets me. The Rock and Roll Hall of Fame is located in Ohio because, as the Cleveland Traveler states, "Well, it's partially because the city was willing to pledge money to it in 1985 when the Rock and Roll Hall of Fame Foundation was deciding on where to build its museum. But the Foundation ultimately decided on Cleveland because of its ties to the early days of rock and roll."

There is an Ohio Historical Marker dated 2003, #46-18, that reads: *When radio station WJW disc jockey Alan Freed (1921-1965) used the term "rock and roll" to describe the up-tempo Black rhythm and blues records he played beginning in 1951, he named a new genre of popular music that appealed to audiences on both sides of 1950's American racial boundaries – and dominated American culture for the rest of the 20th century.*

Was Marty McFly and time travel involved? Because how else could Alan Freed coin a term in 1951 that Maurie Orodenker already used in 1942 in the popular magazine *Billboard*?

Freed was in the first group to be inducted to the Rock and Roll Hall of Fame, along with Elvis Presley, Sam Phillips, Little Richard (ironically Sister Rosetta discovered Little Richard when he was 14 years old; he was singing her songs), Fats Domino, Chuck Berry, Buddy Holly, Jerry Lee Lewis, Ray Charles, Sam Cooke, The Everly Brothers, Robert Johnson, Jimmy Rodgers, and Jimmy Yancey. Not included were Sister Rosetta and Maurie Orodenker.

In December 1938, Sister Rosetta performed with Albert Ammons (on piano) in John Hammond's "From Spirituals To Swing Concert" at Carnegie Hall; *That's All* featured a Little Richard-type piano sound, a Chuck Berry-like guitar riff, and a vocal style that was gritty yet boppin' like Fats Domino. It sounds like rock and roll, and it feels like rock and roll. Here's the thing: if you do the math, it's over a decade before the likes of Ike Turner and Fats Domino even released a record!

Music industry influencers refuse to say that Sister Rosetta is the "inventor of rock and roll." She was inducted into the Rock and Roll Hall of Fame in 2018 as an "Early Influencer." WUNC, a North Carolina Public Radio Station, said, "[Sister Rosetta Tharpe] was the leading figure in birthing rock and roll". On the *Rock Newman Show,* Rock was wowed by Sister Rosetta's story and demanded "from this day forward" she be called, "the real originator."

Let's start at the beginning. Sister Rosetta Tharpe was born Rosetta Nubin on March 20, 1915, in Cotton Plant, Arkansas. Her mother was Katie Bell Nubin, and her father was Willis Atkins. Both her parents picked cotton. Not much else is known about her father, but her mother was a singer, a mandolin player, and an evangelist preacher for the Church of God in Christ, otherwise known as the COGIC. The church encouraged musical expression in worship and allowed women to preach. Her mother was active in music, and included Sister Rosetta from the time she was four years old. She was soon playing the guitar and singing songs like *Jesus Is on the Main Line,* and was known as a "singing and guitar-playing miracle;" her exuberance and talent started at such a young age. She was six years old when her mother left her father and took her on tour. They traveled with an evangelical troupe that did hybrid performances: part sermons, part gospel concerts. Sister Rosetta sat on top of a piano to play her guitar and sing so that people could see her.

In the mid-1920s, Sister Rosetta and her mother settled in Chicago where they continued to perform religious concerts at the COGIC church and occasionally traveled to perform at church conventions throughout the country. Because of all that time on the road and her connection to the church, Sister Rosetta developed fame as a musical prodigy. She stood out in an era when prominent Black female guitarists remained rare.

When Sister Rosetta was 19 years old, her mother decided it was time her daughter got married and set her up with Reverend Thomas Thorpe. The marriage didn't work out. He used her to make money and get more people to come to his church, and Sister Rosetta was not happy. They separated after four years, and mother and daughter moved to New York. Sister Rosetta decided to kinda keep her married last name; she changed the Thorpe to Tharpe, becoming Sister Rosetta Tharpe for the rest of her life.

Sister Rosetta unintentionally started drifting from the church community even as she spread gospel music beyond church walls. At first, her church revival fans thought she "was off"; they were hurt because Sister Rosetta was "theirs", but they were soon won over by her success in the secular world. Performing gospel not in a church setting, with secular audiences, was weird in religious circles. Churchgoers were shocked by the mixture of gospel-based lyrics and secular music, and that gospel was sung in the secular world. It bothered some people that a "church lady" was the mother of rock and roll. But for as many people who didn't like it, there were lots more that did. Sister Rosetta continued performing at different locations outside of the church, strengthening her fame.

So how did Sister Rosetta get her first record deal? In 1938, when Sister Rosetta moved to New York City, she signed with Decca Records. She was the first gospel musician to sign a recording contract. Backed by Lucky Millinder's jazz orchestra, she recorded four songs for Decca: *Rock Me, That's All, The Man and I,* and *The Lonesome Road.* All four of these recordings became instant hits. Sister Rosetta was the nation's first commercially successful gospel singer. *Rock Me* influenced many rock-and-roll singers, like Elvis Presley, Little Richard, and Jerry Lee Lewis.

In New York, she turned some heads and got some powerful people's attention, especially after the 1938 Carnegie Hall "From Spirituals to Swing Concert". It was weird to see a woman as headliner of a music act in any venue; even weirder was that Sister Rosetta performed gospel songs in secular nightclubs alongside blues and jazz musicians and, sometimes, amid scantily clad showgirls. But the weirdest of all (at least to conservative audiences) was a woman playing the electric guitar. According to *Biography,* "The [1938] performance shocked and awed the Carnegie Hall audience."

Sister Rosetta followed up with regular appearances at the Cotton Club where she played and sang with Cab Calloway and Duke Ellington. She was the first Black gospel performer to play for white-only audiences. In 1939, she was in *Time* Magazine with the headline, "Singer sings same songs in church and nightclub."

Some musicians were inspired by her voice, by her soul, by her energy, by her blend of genres, but many musicians were inspired by the way she played the guitar. Sister Rosetta strummed using the ancestor to the "windmill" technique. It's a technique that is often thought to have started with either Pete Townshend or Keith Richards but, um, no. Sister Rosetta had been playing like that for decades. It's described by Michael Ross as, "She slams a chord and waves her arm back and forth in a move that's simultaneously testifying AND directing the chords [to] repeatedly bend notes like a choir director's baton."

It's been suggested that Sister Rosetta was at odds with Decca Records not long after she was signed. Roxie Moore remembers, "Rosetta and Millinder were increasingly at odds in 1943, as Rosetta itched to quit the big-band circuit and renew her career as a strictly gospel act . . . She hadn't wanted to do light fare poking fun at old-time religion or worldly material like 'Tall Skinny Papa', but found herself bound by contractual obligations . . . What we'd call the pop love songs, Sister didn't wanna do, but her record company wanted her to."

Sister Rosetta was on the road for most of the 1940s. She started the decade at 25 years old, rating among the most popular musicians of the day; she was gospel's first superstar. The gal crossed the lines of music genres and male-dominance, and she crossed color lines – all a wonderful rarity. She headlined tours with white and Black artists on the roster. The 2011 BBC documentary *The Godmother of Rock & Roll: Sister Rosetta Tharpe* talked about her touring with The Dixie Hummingbirds and The Jordanaires. Sister Rosetta had a bus with her name on it, and many times the Black artists on the tours slept on her bus because hotels wouldn't allow them in due to the same segregation and racism that prevailed in restaurants and public restrooms.

Sister Rosetta's adventures on tour prompted the song, *Strange Things Happening Every Day*. The song, reflecting the odd segregation of the road, is a wonderful mix of jazz piano, electric guitar, and gospel put to a bouncing beat. It was the biggest hit of her career. It was later covered by Johnny Cash, Tom Jones, and Etta James.

In the mid-1940s, Sister Rosetta had a musical breakthrough, teaming up with blues pianist Sammy Price to record music featuring a combination of piano, guitar, and gospel. The duo's two most famous tracks were *Strange Things Happening Every Day* and *Two Little Fishes and Five Loaves of Bread*.

In 1946, Sister Rosetta saw Marie Knight perform at a Mahalia Jackson concert in New York; she recognized a special talent in Marie. Two weeks later, she showed up at Marie's doorstep to invite her to go on the road. It was a brave and daring move, because it was not the norm for two women to be on the stage without a man; it was even odder for two women to be on tour without a man. Sister Rosetta and Marie toured the gospel circuit as a duo for years. Marie sang and played the piano, and Sister Rosetta sang and played her electric guitar, recording the hits *Up Above My Head* and *Gospel Train*.

Sister Rosetta had dated both men and women in the past; their friends often said they were lovers. It was never publicly announced because it would ruin their careers, which were already strained because they were Black women touring without any men.

Unfortunately, in 1949 their popularity took a sudden downturn. To commemorate Sister Rosetta's first anniversary of being a Virginia homeowner, she put on a concert at what is now the Altria Theater. Supporting her for that concert were the Twilight Singers, who later became known as The Rosettes.

In 1950 Marie and Sister Rosetta performed at Griffith Stadium in Washington, D.C. The concert did well, and Sister Rosetta's promoters, Irvin and Izzy Felds, were planning for a second show. However, Marie had been harboring a desire to break free as a solo act into popular music, and then tragedy happened. Marie's mother and two small children were killed in a fire. She was heartbroken. Sister Rosetta and Marie officially broke up, but still performed together from time to time.

After their breakup, Irvin had the idea to make the second concert include a wedding: Sister Rosetta's! The Felds would promote it, but was up to Sister Rosetta to find a husband.

Tickets went on sale to the public; Sister Rosetta met Russell Morrison – husband found! Russell loved the music industry but couldn't sing or play, but he would later become Sister Rosetta's manager. The wedding was elaborate. People brought wedding gifts, there were massive fireworks after, and about 25,000 people were in attendance. A record was released of the ceremony and concert. Marie Knight was Sister's maid of honor, and her backup singers, The Rosettes, were her bridesmaids. Lucky Millinder, who'd been with Sister Rosetta since the beginning at Decca Records, was Russell's best man. The bride was beautiful, and the evening was a success; somehow no one realized how weird it all was. Sister Rosetta had that way with people: she made them feel comfortable, welcomed, and family – even if it with a ticket price.

As Stevie Wonder would later write in a song, what followed was "seven years of bad luck." Sister Rosetta fell to the back burner for a while. She didn't have any new content, and her songs were considered old. Her songs grew less popular, and she had no gigs. She moved into a row house in Philadelphia and lived a quiet life for a while.

Then in 1957, a man by the name of Chris Barber remembered Sister Rosetta and asked her to tour Europe with him and his band. They toured together for a month, and they were a huge hit. Gospel and rock and roll hadn't traveled to Europe yet, and Sister Rosetta was their early introduction. She was a sensation. She quickly stole the spotlight, but Barber and his band didn't mind.

In 1964, folk revival was on its way to its peak. Sister Rosetta was booked as part of the Folk Blues and Gospel Caravan tour throughout England. During that tour, she did a special nationwide broadcast concert for Granada television. The concert was at the unused railway station at Wilbraham Road, Manchester. Arriving in a horse-drawn carriage, Sister Rosetta played on the train's platform. Across the tracks were stands filled with hundreds of young people. It was cold and rainy, and so she opened with her song *Didn't It Rain* before playing *This Train*.

Bob Dylan, who you might remember started in folk music (he was booed for turning to electric guitar), said, "I'm sure there are a lot of young English guys who picked up electric guitars after getting a look at her." I mean, Dylan did. Dylan was a big fan of Sister Rosetta. He said on his *Theme Time Radio Hour*, "Sister Rosetta Tharpe was anything but ordinary and plain. She was a big, good-lookin' woman, and divine, not to mention sublime and splendid. She was a powerful force of nature. A guitar-playin', singin' evangelist."

If you are interested, Sister Rosetta's railway performance from 1964 is on YouTube. It's amazing.

While she was touring in Europe, her mother grew frail and died. Sister Rosetta toured Europe for a few more years, then she fell ill and returned to America. She suffered a stroke. While in the hospital, doctors found spots on her feet that turned out to be prolonged and untreated diabetes; she had to have a leg amputated. Still, Sister Rosetta talked to family and friends about making a big comeback, but she had a second stroke and passed away a few days later. Sister Rosetta Tharpe was only 58 years old when she died on October 9, 1973, in Philadelphia, Pennsylvania.

Now here's the heartbreaking bit. Even though Sister Rosetta was loved by European audiences for over 20 years, American audiences had forgotten about her. Her funeral was said to be half full. When she was buried at Northwood Cemetery, Sister Rosetta Tharpe was buried without a gravestone marker. She nearly vanished into obscurity.

Then in 1998, Sister Rosetta was honored with a postage stamp. In 2003, there was a tribute album made of her songs featuring Bonnie Raitt, Joan Osborne, and Sweet Honey in the Rock. And, in 2007, she was inducted into the Blues Hall of Fame. The major champion of Sister Rosetta's legacy is Gayle Wald, the author of *Shout, Sister, Shout!* (2008). Because of Gayle's extensive research and TV appearances, the BBC made the 2011 documentary about Sister Rosetta that also aired on PBS American Masters. Bob Merz, a writer in Pennsylvania, saw Gayle in an interview and was taken aback by Sister Rosetta's story – so much so that he organized a benefit concert to pay for a gravestone. This resurgence of the Sister Rosetta legacy just might be why Sister Rosetta Tharpe was finally inducted into the Rock and Roll Hall of Fame as an "Early Influencer" in 2018.

Sister Rosetta's #historymatters because she gave us Elvis' sound, Chuck Berry's guitar style, Aretha Franklin's performance style, Johnny Cash's blend of gospel and folk, and the existence of rock and roll. When you see Sister Rosetta perform, she is the embodiment of rock and roll. She gave us EVERYTHING when she performed; she never held back. You got all of her, in her voice, in her guitar playing, in the energy she gave you: more than anything that's what makes her the inventor of rock and roll, because rock and roll is about how it makes you feel.

It also helps if you can do math.

Innocence Lost by Donavan Barrier

I tried to kill the child inside me.
I did everything I could ever think to do.
I beat him, strangled him, cut him into pieces.
I even tried alcohol poisoning and burying him alive.
No matter what I did, though, he still was there.
He always showed up wherever I went.
He'd stand there, his eyes drowning in salty tears,
Snot rivers plummeting down his face.
Afraid at who he gazed upon.
Me.
I don't know how I can make him stop.
Homicide sure as hell didn't work.
Someone said maybe I should give him a hug
What the hell? I tried everything else.
It wouldn't hurt to give it a shot.
As long as he stops fucking crying, I'll be happy to do that.

Uhura by Dr. Leah Leach

You sat in that chair
For us girls everywhere
You listened to our voices
And tried to understand our choices
Your story may not have been told
But you made us feel bold

At Dachau: The Crematorium by Chuck Kellum 🌍

Here incessant fires burned
Fiercely, in prolonged drudgery,
No mercy:
Regimented cruelty, suffering
And death
Reduced and sanitized
In a fury of flames
As powerful guards barked harsh words and meted abuse,

Exhausted prisoners toiled in muted despair,
Silent ruined bodies piled up in an ever-growing heap,
And above it all,
In anguished sorrow for mankind,
Hovering souls screamed.

I stand before the quiet
Of the long-abandoned ovens

And close my eyes.

Thinking of those who were here:
The tormentors, the tormented,
All the ones with eyes gone blank,

And the others, too . . .

I hear echoes
                    And questions
That penetrate
And emanate
At my core,

And feel compelled

To stay

And listen.

On Working Orientation at a Civil War Reenactment by Sarah E.
Morin

Time-traveler, enter here.
Remember.
See yourself in history.
Reflect.
Forget these
phones, TVs, cars,
but remember ancestors fighting
brother against brother.
Nation unraveling.
Blue and grey
uniforms.

Bloodied pale hands.
Dark wrists enchained,
grasping freedom.
Remember:
yesterday and today,
North and South,
black and white.
Cross borders.
Connect.
Borders 'cross
white and black,
South and North,
today and yesterday.
Remember
freedom. Grasping,
enchained wrists. Dark
hands, pale. Bloodied
uniforms,
grey and blue.
Unraveling nation.
Brother against brother,
fighting ancestors. Remember, but
cars, TVs, phones:
these forget.
Reflect
history in yourself. See.
Remember.
Enter here, time-traveler.

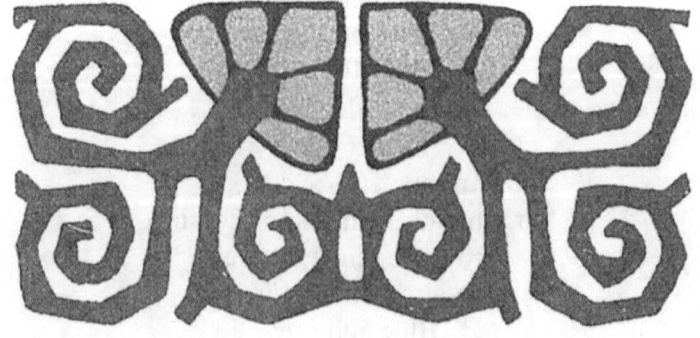

Late Summer by Alison Harlos

Proverbials: Before Roe v. Wade by Vivianne Belle

Knowledge can hit like the proverbial sledgehammer
and it hit her at fifteen years like a physical blow
to both gut and head, wielding trauma and reality
and truth and self-loathing and hatred
 for the (unemployed) boy(friend)-not-yet-a-man
   he lived in a baseballed bedroom in his parents' home
   she lived in her princessed room in her parents' home
yes hatred for him with whom
love on a proverbial hot summer night
meant teenaged hormones raged in consent
but now love is
a purple-green-yellow red-raw bruising to her soul
after a test then another and a third
yielded a literal and proverbial fact of life
in positive blue chemistry
to this (unemployed) girl(friend)-not-yet-a-woman
and because of secrets and fear
   I can't tell my parents he said
   and she replied *I can't tell mine eithe*r
   so he gives her $50 then stops
   returning her calls and avoids eye contact at school
and so now there's also shame
of being a proverbial fool on a Friday night
then her solo Quest To Fix Things
begins with a visit to the one person she thinks
will understand and maybe help and
   Grandma hugs her scared beggaring self
   and gives the money to go to a hush-hush Place
and so she goes alone on a bus
then skittering through unfamiliar streets
finding the proverbially dingy-looking
Place and endures the unendurable
hearing her own proverbial cries of agony
then towels are shoved against her
still crying bent over double as they say
   you can leave in fifteen minutes
   and she leaves on rubber legs
then from the cracks and crevices of her secret

blood runs down and out of her body and
into first pads then the public toilets
she lurches into on those streets she now knows
she'll never forget
       because they'll haunt her dreams with dirty
       familiarity for the rest of her life
bleeding still and silent crying on the painful bus ride
back from that Place where hygiene and health
and safety somehow time warped to the proverbial Dark Ages
where yes her secret was removed
but so was her chance
to ever be a mother.

I Evoke Great Mother by Dr. Leah Leach 🌍

Tribal Connections by Donavan Barrier

You claim yourself as my brother through the blood and lands we're descended from.
You and I have a bond that no human or nation can break.
You take my hand and say that we must stick together as kin.
For our people to survive, we must be as one, united.
But I don't know you.
I've never met you nor seen you before.
Hell, I didn't know you existed until, quite literally, two minutes ago.
Brothers? No, we're not. Family? We've never been.
You're not even a friend or acquaintance.
You're a stranger!
I'm sorry, but that's the plain cold truth.
How can we be close if we lack knowledge of each other?
A tribe is not built solely on just blood and geography.
It's through handshakes, proximity, commonality, geniality.
None of these have we ever shared with each other, my 'brother'.
So please don't say that we have a link.
We don't. That's the long and short of it.
But, I will say I'm open to the possibility.
I'm willing to create some ties between us, though.
So how about we start over, and you tell me your name?

The Promise by Dorothy Lorant

It was your hand I held when we walked thru the woods, a very short way from our door.
You showed me the den where the fox hid her kits … and jack-in-the-pulpit grew

hidden, secure.
The small brown shed where tools and mowers lay you said was the abode of bears,
and to this day my child's mind smiles to think them there.
Yours was the I lap I sat on as you read 'til I slept, to dream of a golden phoenix

who could rise from the flames unscathed.
From you I learned that mermaids were real, and carpets could fly, that a Psammead

(ill-tempered and surly when woken up early!) granted wishes malicious and sly.

And you promised me … you crossed your heart … that you would
never leave me. You
taught me to swim and to sail, to tie a strong knot, to never complain of the wind's icy bite.
And if I misjudged the way to the shore, to stay with my overturned sloop thru the night.
You taught me to dive and to fish, to bait my own hook, to gut my own catch … but never to cook!
   Allowed me to read whatever I chose … of golden apples and Trojan kings,

of far-off lands and wondrous things.
Of vengeful Medea who murdered her young. Of Lavinia bereft of her hands and her tongue.
   You said never back down when I knew I was right. When to walk away … not the same as take flight.   That the arrogant, pedantic, repressive, unkind, would always be thus …

to leave them behind … and let my mind soar.
When the nuns called to complain I had strayed from the mold, you just smiled and replied,
   "She's intrepid … not bold!"   And Mother Superior would retreat to the convent,

convinced I was doomed, with a father *so* indulgent.

And you promised me ... you crossed your heart that you would never
leave me When
I left for college you sent little treats found in some dusty shop on some
obscure street. Rings
made of elephant hair, old books of sonnets, lockets with photos of
ladies in bonnets.

And when I set out for Egypt *alone*, to gaze at the Sphinx and sail on
the Nile, to travel by camel across desert sand ... to wander the souk ...
only *you* understand,

that only **alone** can I traverse this land.
Only you comprehended all that it took to meet Ramses and Ptolemy,
Cleo and Tut. Every sorrow, every pain, every triumph, every gain, was
shared first with you.

And when I married and had a girl-child, *I felt joy for I knew ...*
One day I'd walk thru the woods behind *both of you*
And *her* hand would be in yours, as mine had been too.
You would show her the den of the fox and her kits . . .
And the house where the bears lived, high on a ridge.
Warn her, "Walk softly! Make not a sound!
For a family of trolls lives under this bridge!" ...
For her you would sing and teach her to whistle ... tell her stories of
Psammeads who really existed ... and let her read Poe, no matter how
twisted.
You would show her a world where animals spoke.
Where by day Penelope wove a fine cloak, and stealthily, secretly
unwove it at night.
Where droll Rumpelstiltskin lived gleefully sure his name could never
be guessed, try though they might!
And a lion would remember with awe, kind-hearted Androcles, who
took a thorn from its paw.
And you promised me ... you crossed your heart ... that you would
never leave me.
But on a Sunday in Autumn you wandered away, quietly, softly, where
I could not
follow. And you left me bereft with a terrible sorrow, beyond tears.
For all that I cherished of magic and lore, of honor and goodness and
sweetness of soul, had quietly, softly, perished with you.
And that's when I knew that "I will never leave you" was a promise
untrue.

Choosing by John R Hinton

I begin at the end
I emerge –
From my mother's womb of death
Transformed from a carefree child into
Adult and authority at age eleven
I come from pain –
Sculpted by the chisel of my father's grief
My identity becoming more discernible
An effigy of forced maturation
I evolve –
From torment to tormented to realization
I may choose a different mother than death
A different father than agony
I can choose rebirth –
Agency is the crowning of my imminent arrival
If I choose to accept light instead of darkness
My mother, Love
My father, Hope

Multicultural Family by Mairéad Lewis 🌍

The Legacy of Two Lights by JAC 🌐

Light Two grinding to survive
Light One working to thrive

each limb beautiful and strong
both passing down histories long

Two of blood German and Irish
One of blood Macedonian and French

decades ago, the war called for violence
from a land of Two's origin
forcing One to flee at once
to a land often seen as free to sin

with One's hands waving to those who remained
soon to be lost, never to be found
Two, too, was in the land of the money bound
bringing about tales often stained

Two was full of boisterous singers
mathematicians and builders
seeking to survive their constant grinds
Two brought the lives of ten kinds

One brought the lives of four kin
all fourteen with stars who shine
eventually, a star from One and Two came to meet
bringing the fire that made me

The House By The Sea by Dorothy Lorant

The happiest house I lived in looked out on the sea. Built by carpenters who built ships when sailing was gainful employment and built houses when sailing was slow, the house by the sea never crested a wave on the Atlantic, but she was nevertheless as sea-worthy as any brigantine or whaler. She had endured over 300 years on the coast, low in silhouette, stubborn, defiant.

No rose or lilac softened her flanks ... only juniper and beach plum could tolerate the sea spray that regularly washed over her. As for trees, there were few; gnarled and misshapen, stunted by the wind into tortured shapes more sculptural than botanical.

I used to imagine that the trees were headstones, markers for all the mariners who went down to the sea in ships ... whalers and schooners, gunboats, and battle-wagons ... never to come home. And at night, when a demented wind blew thru warped branches I thought I could hear the trees whisper their names.

There was no reason I should have been happy there, for life was frangible, and anxiety, like Damocles' sword, sometimes hung over me. And yet, in the house by the sea, where waves lapped granite paths, I knew consummate peace ... or I woke daily to the taste of the sea, a coppery tang upon my tongue. And the clicking of horseshoe crabs in the tidal marsh was like that of old ladies knitting. An acapella chorus thrummed always in the air, the thrusting surge of waves rushing to the shore, followed by a muted susurration as they flowed out again.

Summer was merely a time to be tolerated, a kind of technicolor Disneyland comprising too many people, too much noise. It was winter we waited for, when nothing vied with the raucous cry of the seagull and the plaintive song of the tern. Winter, when contentment was the clasp of a child's hand in mine as we walked an empty beach, ours the only footprints in the sand.

"Good morning, Mr. Sun" we sang every morning, even on days when the sun was, at best, a watery light in a viscous sky. Followed by the same refrain in a gruffer voice, "Good morning, little girl, how are **you** today?" And having made obeisance to a solar deity, we proceeded to walk where beauty reigned equally ... on days the sun shone with a laser-like brilliance, and days so sullen there was no telling where sea ended and sky began. Most days, no matter how cold or relentless the wind, we would walk to the harbor when the fishing boats returned with catches of cod and flounder. Then to the shop where two spinster sisters baked cookies the size of a frisbee. Every day, the sea repaid our love, leaving wondrous offerings on a shore strewn with wreckage cast up by wind and wave. Beauty was everywhere.

In the elegant rainbow trapped in the slimy surface of rubbery kelp . . . in the bleached skeleton of a fish … the iridescent nacre of seashells … the squishing song of sand beneath our feet.

The driftwood we gathered each morning became the stuff of mystery as we wove wondrous tales to imagine from whence it came. The wreckage of a pirate ship, perhaps, that had foundered on far-off shoals, taking its villainous crew to briny depths where only mermaids sang. Or perhaps the rotted remains of a Spanish galleon heavy with Aztec gold that never reached the court of a Spanish king.

"Is the treasure still there?" you would ask, and I'd nod. "In huge oaken chests, girded in iron, guarded by cut-throats with swords."

At night, we would raid our stash of driftwood and, like primitive fire-makers, crouch at the hearth, listening to the spitting, crackling wood, and drinking in the rose and emerald, lavender, and cobalt flames of driftwood that had steeped for months, perhaps years, in the exotic chemistry of the sea.

Sometimes, cocooned in scratchy wool blankets, we would fall asleep by the fire, warm as hibernating bears, as long as the embers lasted. Only close to dawn did we burrow out of our wooly dens and re-light the fire, pushing back the cold that trickled through small chinks and crevices.

And when a nor'easter barreled down the throat of the harbor, all hell would break loose … uprooting small craft anchored in its path. Ripped from their moorings, tossed like toys, the boats piled up in splintered heaps on the beach. To make amends for its fury, after a storm passed, the sea laid treasures at our feet; seaglass burnished smooth, to be gathered and set in glass jars on a sunny windowsill where, like brilliant shards of glass in a kaleidoscope, they cast ever-changing colors on walls and floor. And starfish, that would cling to our hands as tightly as tiny octopi.

Once, an eerie fish, a kind of deep-ocean eel, washed up still alive in a tidal pool. Razor sharp teeth, small malevolent eyes, and frenzied thrashing warned us to leave this hell-fish alone, and hope an imminent high-tide would return it to the deep.

In the decades since house and sea were left behind, our houses became bigger, more polished. Where once I had to place shims under furniture in the house by the sea, to compensate for splintery, foot-wide floorboards that defied alignment, I live now in a house with burnished hardwood floors, meticulously level.

My sanitized, homogenized, pasteurized life no longer suffers a chimney whose 300-year-old bricks need repointing. And my garden is home now to respectable trees in dull, uniform rows. *My gas fireplace is quite realistic and ever so clean!* No ashes blow on the hearth; no embers scorch the rug. *But neither do I ever lay before this hearth at night and listen to the spitting and crackling of driftwood or revel in colors dredged from the sea.*

And more and more often, in unguarded moments, I am ambushed by memories of a house that wrapped its ancient hand-hewed arms around us and sang us to sleep on long winter nights with wind-songs and sea-songs and the keening voices of mariners asleep in the deep.

And more and more often, it is to the house by the sea that I long to return … to its lonely shores and mercurial moods … to its legends of pirates and mermaids … where seaweed has rainbows and the sea tastes of copper.

And happiness was a child's hand clasped in mine.

All Bloomed Out by Mairéad Lewis 🌍

B/W Abstract by Jerry Dreesen

Palm Sunday Tornado (April 11, 1965) by Mike Nierste

red sky at night
sailors delight
red sky in morning
sailors take warning

That morning's first red rays
were beautiful to behold.
A glow, not so scary at first
became a war party
charging over the horizon
in blazing bloodshot war paint
stirring up shrouds of black clouds behind them.

Wind whipped white caps
onto normally quiet waters
transforming Kodachrome colors
to silver halide portraits of funeral processions

84

with mourners dressed in black and white,
which from a distance blended to make those days
gray.

Those first sweet smells of rain
became tastes of storm,
that spiraled up to tornadoes,
then surged to claim names
of people I can't recall,
whose names I never knew.
Two hundred sixty-five died.

Storms shook walls and brought them down
Buildings dissolved like sugar in a coffee cup.
Skies changed from black to green
and back and when this storm subsided,
final phases of squall circled like vultures,
when skies were near
clear.

Fragments of barns and homes
were strewn about, spilled like matchsticks.
Animals, some of whom were human,
lay in fields as well.
Nature, as it turns out, doesn't use only
positive reinforcement to make her point.
Power is often proclaimed in thunderous catastrophe.

Tornadoes are remembered, because they are
listed as a cause of death for so many unknown or forgotten.
What doesn't kill you makes you stronger.
So say some survivors
who scrape up, burn and bury the dead.
Survivors who attempt to put pieces back together,
who check the sky, this time hoping for red sky at night.

A Serendipitous Collision by Patricia Rossi

Amber hues of sunlight filter through my kitchen window. I take one last sip of my coffee, savor its taste, lace up my sneakers, and head outside for my morning run. The perforated paged calendar taped to my refrigerator is haphazardly torn to the month of November. Difficult to fathom. The days have tumbled into months. It seems like just yesterday the towering oaks and maples scattered about the neighborhood were canopies of green, a welcomed reprieve from Mother Nature's scorching summer days. But now, majestic tree boughs are almost bare, sidewalks are a vibrantly colored collection of fallen leaves, in a bold palette of crimson, burnt orange, and golden yellow. This November morning the air is seasonably cool and crisp; the sun has just risen. Quite a glorious sight to behold, the sky is dramatically wrapped in a tangerine velvet.

A bit of personal history, I have always been a runner, an accomplished distance runner, fast enough to place in local marathons and town races. But now the trophies have been relegated to mere dust collectors, the earned medals are old and tarnished, the years and injuries have caught up with me, my pace noticeably slower, and my distance significantly shorter. Nevertheless I have remained determined to start each day still kicking the old asphalt as best I can.

I retired just a few years ago, moved across the United States and settled on the East Coast. As a serious life-long runner, I was initially concerned about the disparities in temperature, diversity of seasons, and terrain. I was accustomed to running in a rather warm climate year-round and navigating much flatter courses; I eventually adjusted.

However, a far greater challenge awaited me: establishing and successfully maintaining a social life, finding friends, making connections. I had enthusiastically embarked upon my moving preparations, held a garage sale, sold my house, donated furniture, and eventually loaded up a van packed with neatly labeled corrugated boxes. I was excited about the prospects of starting a new chapter in my life. I envisioned juggling invites in an overbooked social calendar, with new faces and friends, and endless activities to fill my retired days: perhaps book clubs, luncheons, or sip and paint parties. What was I possibly thinking?

In hindsight, as I busily combed through old household goods and real estate listings, and archived a lifetime of my belongings into color-coded plastic tubs, I also stored away something else . . . denial. Truth be told I am and have always been extremely shy, emergence from my metaphorical shell has been a life-long struggle. Within weeks of my relocation, I found myself in a freshly painted, newly furnished apartment. I was extremely lonely, isolated, severely depressed, and rapidly deteriorating into a retired recluse.

Other than my morning run and the occasional trip to the store I really had no reason to leave my apartment. I spent hours upon hours reading, devouring and finishing one book after another. Admittedly I certainly do enjoy reading, most especially history. For me, running and reading all sorts of history are passionate threads, deeply woven into the fabric of my life. In fact, without much consideration for location or monthly rental payment, I had quickly signed the lease for my new apartment as I was so impressed by its magnificent built-in floor to ceiling bookcases. Additionally, I immediately saw potential in the second bedroom. With an abundance of natural light, I fancied it as my very own library, to be organized alphabetically with my extensive collection of history books. Despite what seemed like a cozy place to call home, the days were long, too quiet, and I felt completely detached from the outside world. But then it happened. My two life passions collided when I literally ran into a local history chapter. The consequences were life-changing.

Early one morning I'd headed out for a run; the neighborhood was blanketed in a thick fog, the sky was varying shades of charcoal, accompanied by a steady drizzle. Inadvertently I ran in a different direction, then turned right after a mile or so, turned left, and continued. I was lost in thought, seriously contemplating packing up and moving again; I felt despondent, hopeless, and alone. Practically in tandem with my sneaker-clad feet striking the pavement came the recurring question, where could I possibly move to? I continued to run and realized I was lost.

There were a series of narrow roads that hugged small cottages. Panic set in, where was I? The streets were concentric circles. I felt like I had fallen into the pages of a story book, perhaps a fairy tale of some sort, until of course I made another sharp right turn and situated directly in front of me was an old cemetery. Weathered gravestones with faded, illegible epitaphs; was I dreaming? Was I hallucinating from lack of social interaction or perhaps from all the history I voraciously read?

Just then I noticed sign-posts indicating landmarks: they denoted the minister's house (circa 1862), a chapel (circa 1864), and an old schoolhouse (circa 1872). It was eerie, yet from an historical perspective so intriguing. I had questions. Who had lived here? What exactly was the history of this community? What about preservation? It was remarkable; completely intact, and museum-like. As the fog lifted, I eventually navigated my way out and ran home. My mysterious discovery weighed heavy as my questions continued to clang in my head. I needed answers. I initially tried to research the area online. After very little success I drove over to the library and looked around for a local history section. I found an inordinate amount of information. I gathered some articles, newspaper clippings, vintage sketches of the area, and some rather large maps, and sat myself down at an old wooden table near the reference librarian and delved in.

It was fascinating. Pieces of this historical puzzle were slowly coming together for me. I learned that with the rise of revivalism in the United States during the 1860s, the community I had stumbled upon was established by an association as a place for religious worship and meetings for New York Methodists, with an average population estimated at about three hundred. However, during special ceremonies and celebrations, all sorts of hymns filled the air and the population rose to almost five thousand! I was intrigued about a house inexplicably designated "the Safe House." More research identified it as part the Underground Railroad!

My head was buried in one of the old maps when I suddenly heard a soft whisper; it was the reference librarian. She smiled and said, "Good afternoon. I see you are studying some local history." I nodded. She continued, "It just occurred to me, our historical preservation society is meeting now, downstairs in Room 125, if you are interested. The elevator and the staircase are to the left of the children's room."

I politely answered, "Thank you," then stuttered, "Oh, I don't know, I would like to, but, oh, I just can't." The librarian's suggestion created heart palpitations for me; I could feel beads of sweat on my forehead. Me, enter a room full of strangers, and introduce myself? Despite the historical enticement, I could not do it. As though she sensed my anxiety was tinged in curiosity, the librarian looked directly at me and said, "Come on, give it a try." Within minutes we were standing outside Room 125. She turned the door's large brass knob as I peered in its half glass window. I considered running back up the staircase, but the door swung open. It was too late. I entered. Coffee percolated on a corner table next to a tower of Styrofoam cups and sliced crumb cake. Local maps, like the ones I had just been perusing, were pinned to a large bulletin board. Old artifacts, pages from Methodists' missals, liturgical books of song and prayer, and authentic mid 1860's garments were encased in glass.

I glanced to my right; my heart skipped a beat. Strategically positioned on large piece of plywood was a miniature model of the community I had stumbled upon that very morning! As an introvert, what an ice-breaker! The room was alive with captivating conversation, the damp vanilla smell of old books, newspapers, and friendly faces. It resonated and excited me; I felt welcomed and began to chat with a few folks.

For the first time since I'd moved, my undeniable feelings of loneliness dissipated. The group was warm, kind, and embracing. Many of them approached me and encouraged me to formally join the historical society. I began to attend events, became an official member, served as a docent, and participated in an oral history project and a variety of re-enactments. My solitary running and interest in local history collided, and provided me with a plethora of social invites and intellectually stimulating opportunities. Exploration into and a shared deep appreciation for days gone by has forged lasting friendships offering camaraderic for the days ahead.

Amazing Grace by Bonita Cox Searle

We drive from our city homes
and meet at the crest of the cemetery
just outside Adelphi
where the Alleghenies reach the end of their line,
and we meet our beginnings.

We are cousins with children grown and
their children, who run around the graves
that slope down the hill,
scattering late autumn leaves across the paths
as they make airplane arms and goofy noises
and poke each other with happy fingers

We gather around the deep square hole that
the caretaker has dug in the dark soil
next to a dozen or so Whites and McBrooms
who wait.

As we pray, I wonder,
What will they think when Dad arrives
in ashes?
No body to rise again
as they were
taught and taught and taught
for two centuries and more.

My father,
the last child of Frank and Maisie
to leave us,
was the different one.
No coalmine or farmer's plow or teacher's life
for him,
with his fingers that danced over a piano
and made it glad to be alive,
and a restless heart that could wound
when it moved.
Is he glad, I wonder, that the long years are over
of trying and trying and trying
to get life right,
to be the man
he thought he should be?

As I stand among my cousins,
who tower over me like the ancient trees
that protect the surrounding hills,
I realize there is no one
between us and death.

The generations before us
rest gentle beneath our feet,
and the generations after us
prepare to let us go
as my daughter's voice flows with Amazing Grace,
and the late afternoon sun pours over us all.

Late Bloomer On The First Of November by Mairéad Lewis 🌎

Late Bloomer by Mairéad Lewis 🌎

windswept delicacies
rare as rubies and strange
like leftover creatures
encased in amber as if
soldiering on
forever
despite the advancing
gales of November

Witching Hour tanka by Alys Caviness-Gober

witching hour haunts me
awakening in darkness
generations gleam
blue eyes and brown eyes shining
carrying love in my world

91

Waiting by Alison Harlos

When you think that you're alone. by Alison Harlos

You probably are.
When you think that you're forgotten
you probably aren't.
It's a long road
for us outspoken folks
the ones with the big mouths.
Sure we can command a room or a conversation
but not our intention
but not our selves.
When you think you are too much
for them, you probably are.
For those that cannot hear beyond your rhetoric of coping
you try to connect
and then it's just too much.
So you try to observe and be quiet.
Remove the mask, they ask
then you Remove your mask, they scatter
when Remove your mask, the chatter.
When you feel you're alone
you're NOT.
There are many like us
we've learned to lurk
on a lonely road
hiding in plain sight.
The ones with the big hearts
with loud voices
why are we crying alone?

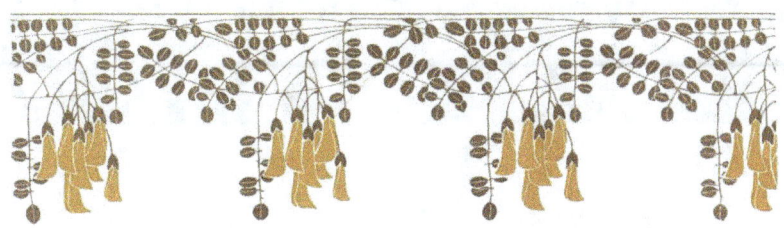

93

Cabin and Autumn Leaves by Sarah E. Morin

The Lover's Plea by Dorothy Lorant

"Seek you the Magdalen woman, Merchant?" the elders asked, their honeyed voices masking glee when I found your house shuttered and silent. "Returned this very day from Samarkand and already rushing to lavish fine raiment and gems on the harlot?"

"She is not here," they jeered. "She left to follow the Nazarene. Besotted with his words, she sits daily at his feet, spellbound by this zealot *who calls God himself his father!"*

"Blasphemy" they spat. "Have nothing to do with the whore!"

And so I hastened to where the Nazarene was preaching and saw you, as they said . . . sitting in the dust,
your beautiful face transfigured with joy,
weeping tears of ecstasy as you clung to every word. Never have you looked thus at me, Mary,
and my mind flinches at the thought that this trivial man
. . . this carpenter . . . this, this *insignificant trickster*
could have beguiled you so utterly.

I watched, then, as you took a vial of precious oil and poured it over the feet of the Nazarene.
And then you dried his feet with your glorious mane of hair as black as ravens' wings.

"They say," a man whispered in my ear,
"that she sold a magnificent blush-pink pearl to buy that oil."
How well I know that gem.   It is the pearl I gave you when first I tasted the incredible sweetness of your body.

You cannot have changed so utterly, my Love! You, who always scorned prophets and priests.
Stripped them of their self-enshrinement with your withering contempt.
You, who despised scribes and Pharisees, swollen with their pompous conceits. How happily you always mocked them . . . these hills re-echoing laughter from your throat like water spilling in to empty jars.

Come back to me, my beloved!
Put this madness aside and be again as you were. Still I dream of the Eden of your arms.
Still I feel the rapture of remembered nights.
I have loved you unaltered since first I saw you at the well, singing some haunting canticle of your own device,
the sound trembling in the air as clear and sweet as a lark at daybreak.

Why do you look at me with pity, Mary?
Me! . . . the richest of merchant princes
whose love can place a world of treasure at your feet!
   Go then, follow the Nazarene!
He is but one more of the poor, deluded oracles who come and go in
Judea, flaring briefly,
then vanishing into obscurity.
This land has always spawned his ilk . . . .
would-be messiahs and magicians, conjurors and charlatans.
   Go then, I will soon forget you,
and if in sleep I sometimes moan your name, it will be by habit only,
not desire.
A momentary thirst I can assuage by turning to another.
Already memory fades . . .
your laughter, your limpid eyes, your silken hair, your curve of cheek
and breast . . . As for the Nazarene, his name will not endure
even to the next harvest,
and those who remember him at all will say, "Whatever happened to
that fool, that Jesus?"
And your name, Mary of Magdala, will be as obscure and forgotten as
his.

Mother Tree - Firsts by Dr. Leah Leach

The Kind Of Song That Humankind Should Sing by Ndaba Sibanda

The artists across the globe got together in song and dance,
and practised and composed a song whose lyrics go like:
when the world seems to cartwheel on you,
when the world seems to tumble on you,
I'm that friend to come to your rescue,
I'm that friend to count on, to lean on,
to put a beam on your face, a great grin,
and delight in your soul, hope every mile
of the way, light in your night, music
in your heart, buoyant, calming remedy
and comedy, for laughter is lovely life.

Together let's pick up the pieces,
together let's pick up the pieces,
life may not be predictably perfect
but let's learn to relish, cherish
and bring around perfect times,
be filled with thankful moments,
and thrive, live in those moments,
and embrace fond reminiscences
of boom, brightness, and blessings.

For the love of love and humanity,
for the love of love and humanity,
let there be a sweet song in our hearts,
a listening pair of ears, a loving pair of hands,
a fragrance on our bodies, a winning smile
on our looks, and joy in our souls, every mile
of the way in our one hopeful human race.

I've been thinking a lot about the optional theme for this year's *The Polk Street Review, #historymatters*. Like the *Introduction* says, it feels relevant because of the ongoing global pandemic and the current cultural and political climate here and abroad. It's a popular hashtag across social media platforms, yet *#historymatters* feels . . . personal.

As this edition of *The Polk Street Review* goes to print, COVID-19 continues to mutate and spread. Indiana still ranks among most dangerous states to be in, due to its low vaccinated percentage (57%). As a disabled-fully-vaccinated-and-boosted-but-still-self-isolating person, I'm grateful to those who are fully vaccinated, those who are also boosted, and those who continue to use protective measures like mask-wearing and social distancing. Their vigilance protects all of us. It's hard to understand that, despite science and historical evidence, there are (still) too many people here in Indiana and across the nation that (still) believe that vaccinations and mask-wearing are MAGA-inspired "freedom" issues rather than real-world health issues. My disgust for those folks runs deep.

Which brings me to a question I face almost every day: *How can I separate my "personal" self from my "public" self as the founder and President of Community • Education • Arts?*

Being a creative soul, I express my thoughts and feelings through Art with a capital A. Like most creatives, I write my feelings, I paint my feelings; we "craft" our feelings in many art forms. When it comes to political isues, my creativity is constantly torn between my personal feelings of outrage and awareness of my public responsibilities. If you know me, you know I'm a liberal left-wing progressive Democrat-voting "woke" anti-Fascist feminist anti-racist LGBTQIA+ ally who believes in equality and human rights FOR ALL.

I've never walked easily upon the fine line that lies delicately between the personal and the public, especially with political issues. So what to "do" with my little 501(c)(3) all-volunteer arts nonprofit when it comes to core values of equality and human rights for all? Well, CEArts has been committed to equality, diversity, inclusion, and access for all since its inception in 2014. However, when George Floyd was murdered on 25 May 2020 by Minneapolis MN police officers, I realized that "my" organization's core values weren't publicly expressed. So, my arts-partner-in-crime Sarah E. Morin and I wrote a *Statement Against Racism* and published it on the CEArts website, and we did several podcast episodes dedicated to discussing discrimination and prejudice against targeted "groups".

Those discussions brought *#historymatters* to the forefront, for the organization and for myself. I noticed that, like CEArts – we weren't the first – many local, state, and national arts organizations became more public as they promoted and adopted IDEA as the guiding principle in their funding imperatives and to address structural inequalities in the arts. IDEA is the acronym for **Inclusion, Diversity, Equity,** and **Access**. The Indiana Arts Commission has a page dedicated to defining IDEA, and I encourage you to read it (just Google "IAC and IDEA").

"My" little 501(c)(3) all-volunteer arts nonprofit is not a political organization, but it is an Arts organization, and history tells us what happens to the Arts, artists, and arts organizations when freedom and democracy are taken away by authoritarian regimes.

#historymatters – and history happens now, right?

Since 24 February 2022, we've watched Ukraine fight against Russian forces for its survival as an independent and democratic country. But how many of us realize that in the 17th century Ukraine was partitioned between Russia and Poland, and ultimately absorbed by the Russian Empire? Or that after the Russian Revolution during WWI, a Ukrainian national movement formed the Ukrainian People's Republic? How many of us know it only lasted from 1917-1922 because in 1922 Ukraine was **forced** to become a founding member of the Soviet Union? How many of us know that in 1991 Ukraine **regained** its independence from the Soviet Union after the Soviet Union collapsed? How many of us know that since 20 February 2014 Ukraine has **continuously** fought off Russia incursions? That means Ukraine's latest war for independence has already been going on for eight years and counting, friends, eight years and counting. Sitting here in our comfortable lives in America's Heartland, can we really appreciate what it's like to live in a war zone? Imagine what it would be like for us – ordinary citizens – to literally fight alongside our miltary troops? To fight not "just" for democracy and our country, but for our life, our loved ones' lives, for our homes, businesses, schools, churches, for our very freedoms and rights? **For over eight years?** Can we even begin to comprehend what living like would be like?

In the United States, our forbearers fought for and achieved a democracy that protected democratic ideals like separation of church and state, desegregation, voting rights for non-whites and women, body-autonomy rights for women, and marriage equality rights for LBGTQIA+ couples. Yet we find ourselves in a time when those battles must be fought once again. *#historymatters* here and now, and I can't separate the public from the personal regarding fundamental freedoms and human rights: "my" organization and I stand for equality for all.

Some of my friends and family have already advised me not to publicly "go all political" because it will "hurt" my public self as an individual artist and as President of CEArts. They mean that if I publicly speak out on "political issues", it will hurt art sales for me personally, and it will hurt arts support for and participation in CEArts events and opportunities.

If, as an individual artist, I lose art sales because I express my political opinons, so be it.

As President of CEArts – an organization offering two annual literature-based projects, *The Polk Street Review* and *Noblesville Interdisciplinary Creativity Expo* (NICE) – well, "my" organization is literally named *Community • Education • Arts*! How can I **not** speak out publicly against politics that negatively affect community, education, and the Arts? One of the most horrifying political indications that *#historymatters* **right now** is that right-wing faux-Christian extremists on library boards and school boards in Indiana and across the nation are **banning books**, which history tells us is a significant step on the path of Fascism.

Ordinary Americans have fought and died for independence, religious freedom, democracy, and Civil Rights for all Americans. Ordinary Americans – the Greatest Generation – famously defeated Fascism in

WWII when thousands fought and died to protect American democracy from things like books bans and denying freedom and human rights to certain groups of people. But, yes, in 2023, right-wing extremist faux-Christians in America are banning books and stripping away freedom and human rights from certain groups of people. Acoss our country, that kind of political authoritarian faux-Christian extremism is slithering into our our community libraries, our education system, our Arts. Thus it is that I find the theme of this book to be one of public consciousness and awareness, yet also poignant and personal. #historymatters throughout our past, our present, and out future. It is then, it is now, and it is yet to be what we make it.

On 24 April 2022, comedian Jon Stewart accepted *The Mark Twain Prize for American Humor*. I watched his acceptance speech several times on YouTube. Now, I'm no Jon Stewart, but I take courage from the fact that public figures in the Arts like him **do** speak out about their own political views.

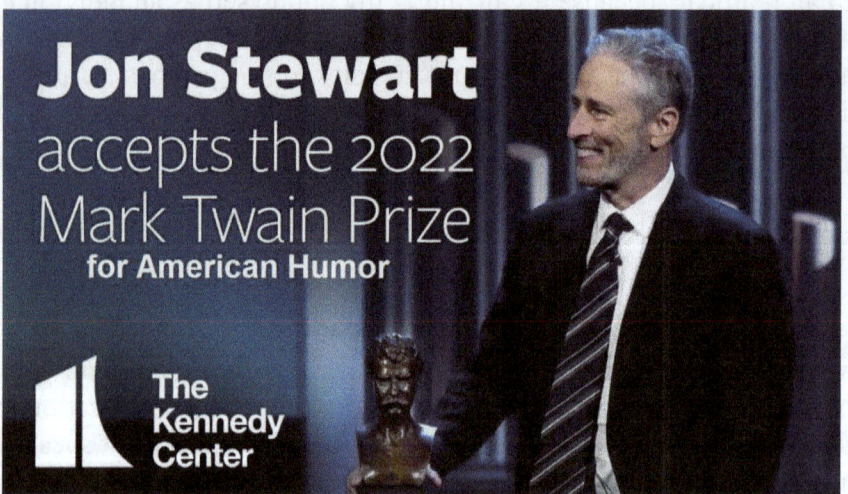

I hope you will understand that I believe it's important to speak out, to protest, to work in any way you can to help create the kind of world you want for your children and grandchildren. Most days, like most folks, I feel like there's not a lot I can do, because, like most ordinary Americans, I'm just one person living in a small town. I rail on social media; I vote; I write protest poetry and prose: my political imprint – my soapbox – is small.

I can't think of a better way to end this essay than with some words from Stewart's acceptance speech, which remind us that, indeed, *#historymatters*:

It's not the woke police that are gonna be an existential threat to comedy, it's not The Fresh Prince, it's the Crown Prince. It's not the fragility of audiences, it's the fragility of leaders. ... Comedy doesn't change the world, but it's a bellweather. ... When a society is under threat, comedians are the ones who get sent away first. It's just a reminder to people that democracy is under threat. Authoritarians are the threat to comedy, to music, to thought, to poetry, to progress, to all those things. ... It ain't the pronoun police, it's the secret police – it always has been and it always will be. . . . (Stewart points to the Mark Twain award statue) *and this man's decapitated visage is a reminder to all of us that what we have is fragile and precious, and the way to guard against it isn't to change how audiences think, it's to change how leaders lead.*

Think about Jon Stewart's words, and how important our democracy actually is to our own lives – every single one of us can change how our leaders lead **if we vote for candidates** who will lead with honesty, integrity, and are committed to equal rights for all of us. We must all commit to democracy, and be on the right side of history for our children and grandchildren.

103

2023 *The Polk Street Review* Awards

Award of Merit (*Best in Book*):
The 2023 *Award of Merit* goes to Donavan Barrier for his thought-provoking poem, *Tribal Connections*. We love the distinct angle and conversational tone addressing difficult realities. It's a wonderful poetic expression of processing emotions: moving from feelings of difference, distance, and negativity to a willingness to reach out.

Special Award:
Special Awards are given when we feel a submitter, or a particular piece, has somehow resonated something that takes us out of a normal category award. Our 2023 *Special Award* goes to Dorothy Lorant! All of her submissions (*The House By The Sea, The Suicide, The Waters of Lethe, The Promise, The Lover's Plea*) resonated with us as powerful storytelling with a variety of thematic interests and subject matter. Each piece evoked a unique sense of time and place, and they take the reader on interesting journeys.

2023 TPSR Category Awards

Artwork Images:

First Place: **Still Looking Good 2** by Jerry Dreesen
Second Place: **Late Summer** by Alison Harlos
Third Place: **All Chains Are Equal** by Mairéad Lewis

Prose:

First Place: **Hiraeth for the Holidays** by Jeff Couch
Second Place: **Excerpts from *Journey to the West 1840*** by Jean Roberts
Third Place: **A Serendipitous Collision** by Patricia Rossi

Poetry/Lyric:

First Place: **Autopsy of Prometheus** by Rue Sparks
Second Place: **Palm Sunday Tornado (April 11, 1965)** by Mike Nierste
Third Place: **Alone with this rambling mind** by Alison Harlos

2022 Noblesville Interdisciplinary Creativity Expo (NICE)

Noblesville Interdisciplinary Creativity Expo (NICE) is our annual classic literature-based project, and we've decided to start including it in our annual anthology, *The Polk Street Review*. Each year, we select four works of classic literature and one passage from each book, and we podcast our "deep dive" discussions of "the good, the bad, and the ugly" of them. Creatives of all kinds submit any kind of artwork inspired by either each work as a whole or the standalone passages.

The 2022 NICE project's four works of classic literature were: ***The Story of an Hour*** by Kate Chopin (1894, 1895); ***The Lottery*** by Shirley Jackson (1948); ***A Passage To India*** by E.M. Forster (1924); ***Midnight In The Garden of Good and Evil*** by John Berendt (1994).

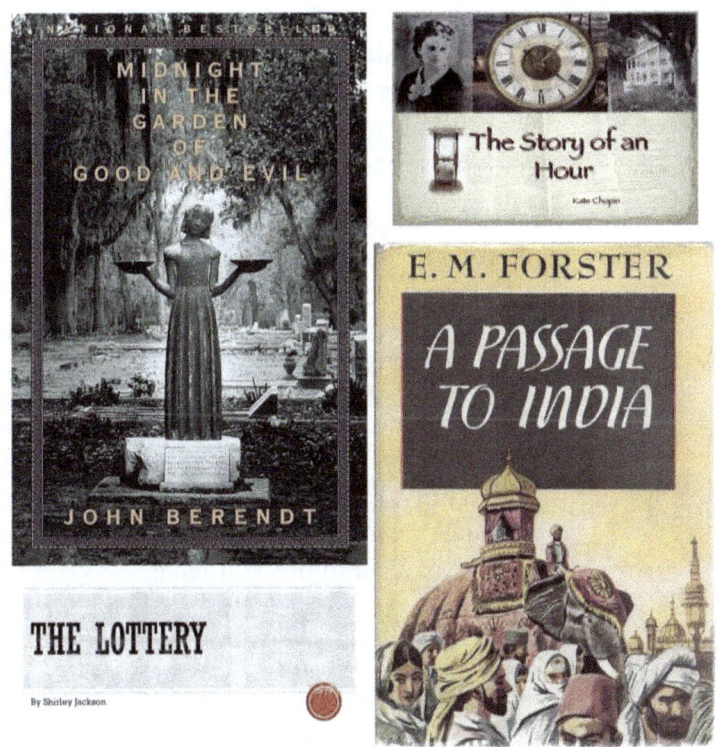

You can read the four standalone passages at:
https://cearts.org/2022-nice

Here are 2022 NICE pieces:
Inspired by *The Story of an Hour* by Kate Chopin:

Sunday Ham by Nancy Simmonds

Anna the nervous new bride
wished to serve Sunday dinner with pride
asked her mama-in-law
in hopes she would thaw
her disfavor and act as a guide.

Anna placed that big ham in the pan
to roast while she stirred up the flan.
Mama grabbed a big knife
took a helluva swipe
sliced the end off that ham in the pan.

Then she basted, arranged it just so
for back in the oven to go.
Anna said with a frown,
"Though I grew up downtown,
why cut that whole part into two?"

Mama put her jewel'd hand to her chin
replied with a touch of chagrin,
"When I was but a lass
Madre cut that crevasse
as was taught by her mum, Catherine."

As Anna served dinner that date
four generations pulled up a plate
then she bravely asked, "Dears,
I've been wondering here
why two odd sized ham pieces I bake?"

Mama turned to question Madre
who in turn looked to Cath'rine to say,
"When we bake Sunday ham
slice it once in the pan
what's the reason we bake it this way?"

Now old Catherine laughed with a wheeze
shook her head and answered with ease
"When Mom taught me to cook

our home was 'naught but nook.
Our one roaster was too small for to squeeze

a reg'lar sized ham in one piece
so we cut it in two or in threes.
When she got her own home
my gal took the tradition I own
and kept it without analysis."

The moral of this tale is true
if you think to follow a rule
before blindly accepting
take the chance on a quest'ning
and reduce acting out like a fool.

This Hour by Alys Caviness-Gober

Unavoidable fingers of purple and yellow
grasping at her, creeping out of this sky,
reaching down within scentlets of wisteria and
dandelion, trilling from choking throats of cicadas
and songbirds;

first, in all too familiar terror,
she tries to beat them back, wearing
all too familiar armor
battered by years of battle, years of withstanding,
and then

she lets go
and the armor falls away
and she is purple and yellow
like a bruise and a blossom and
her breath is sweetened
like wisteria and dandelion
and her choked throat opens
as she throws out her arms
wide welcoming tomorrow
and whispers with monstrous joy,
free
free
free!

Inspired by *The Lottery* by Shirley Jackson:

The Parallel by Nancy Simmonds

Between fare and well I leave thee
Eyes too dim to see thee.
I can but only hear your sigh
and mine.
My final breath
gently stirs the veil
'tween this fraught-filled life
and one unknown beyond.
My feeble fingers lose their gentle touch
upon your own.
I hear your sigh.
Your cry fades into
an abundant silence
my abundance now
a parallel to yours.

The Box by Alys Caviness-Gober

Old wooden boxes never forget
the items they held
the places they rested
the people who made
and carried them;

they smell of things
leathery and hard
acrid and musty
the scrapings of good
and evil;

they grow shabbier as their paint
splinters and cracks
fading into the color of the wood
that now stains
like blood.

Inspired by *A Passage to India* by E.M. Forster:

An Eternity in Gol Gumbaz by Nancy Simmonds

Gol Gumbaz and its aged dome
draws its share of tourists to this dead space
not to honor the sultan or his women
moldering here for generations
but to play in the architecture
cool under the equatorial sun
to walk between the cenotaphs.

This mausoleum was designed
to honor the sultan's women
curved like a hip or breast
a shoulder, a brow
the crown of the head
of his youngest wife
his older wife
his favorite mistress
his daughter.
He could not face eternity
without them buried near.

Climbing the long stone stairs to the gallery above
here is where the true memorial lies.
Whisper on one side of the massive dome
and those soft and secret words are heard clearly
on the other side.
Giggling schoolgirls divide to try the game
couples too to stand across the way
to listen for the voices of their friends
their lovers
whispering in their ears
eavesdropping on what others say
sharing silliness
sharing secrets
echoing the soft sounds the ruler so loved to hear.

When the guards shuffle through one last time
when the guides and tourists leave
when the sunsets fade

and the birds fly home
when the moon rises
and the bats come out to feed
the ghost of the sultan relaxes in his tomb
and smiles his eternal smile
as the whispering begins
between his youngest wife
his older wife
his favorite mistress
and his daughter.
Whispers slide across the dome
the stone sky his dead eyes see
and he smiles
holding his women close.

In A Mirabar Cave by Alys Caviness-Gober

Unlike the exquisite echoes of certain places
    – like Gol Gumbaz in Bijapur, where even faintest whispers
    circle seven times
    or Echo Point in Mandu, where even long solid sentences
    depart and return unbroken –
unlike those perfect phenomena,
the echo in a Marabar cave is devoid of distinction.
Shouts and murmurs, whispered hopes
and prayers, polite niceties and not-so-polite
noseblowings, boot squeaks and match strikes,
and even pleasingly hushed conversations
all reverberate with a lifelessness
a monotony quivering dully, up and down its walls,
    – like eternally watchful little worms coiling 'round
    yet unable to complete their unspeakable circles –
their tedious toiling builds,
as when several people talk at once,
becoming a howling overlapping noise
echoes generating echoes and the cave becomes filled
stuffed with a snake made of little worms
all writhing independently yet moving as one
    – such is the echoingly banal *boum*
    in a Mirabar cave.

Inspired by *Midnight In The Garden Of Good And Evil* by John
Berendt:

Two Views at a Crossroads by Nancy Simmonds

MawMaw is dying.
Her shrinking world is a small room
dressed in faded wallpaper.
Gauze curtains at the windows mute the light
like the cataracts across her eyes.

Aunt Gin has removed the photographs from their frames
that she may hold them close
in her knobby knuckled hands:
PawPaw so young and handsome on their wedding day,
Roscoe solemn in his uniform of war,

Sadie in satin.
Smiling.

MawMaw's face softens
as she touches Sadie's smile with shaking fingers.
She was a dancer, she said, just like you.

Mama tightens her lips,
hardens her eyes.
She was a jailbird, kid.
Didn't amount to nothin'.

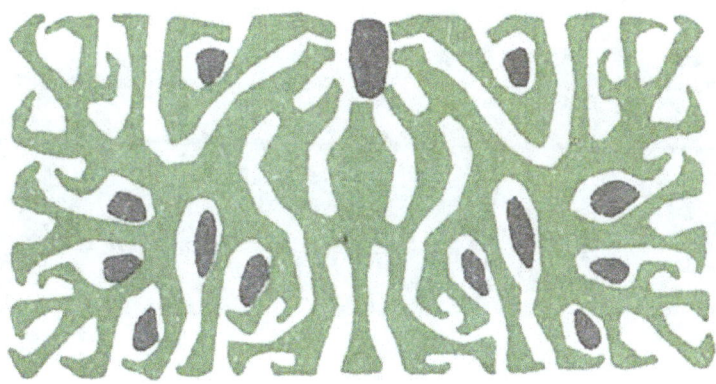

The Color of Old Newspapers by Alys Caviness-Gober

Yellowed pages
– from the *Savannah Morning News*, April 2, 1914 –
line the old wooden chest
and I lift the lid to read:

> *TANGO IS NO SIGN OF INSANITY, HOLDS JURY*
> *DECIDES THAT SADIE JEFFERSON IS NOT INSANE*
> *It is no indication of insanity to tango. This*
> *was settled yesterday by a lunacy commission*
> *which decided that Sadie Jefferson is sane. It*
> *was alleged that the woman tangoed all the way to*
> *police headquarters recently when she was*
> *arrested.*

and I laugh because it's funny to me
– that the tango could even be considered an insanity –
– that there was an actual *lunacy commission* –
and I laugh with vicarious joy visualizing Sadie Jefferson
– whoever she was –
gloriously tangoing all the way to police headquarters
– *my god, how far was it?!* –
but then . . .
my privileged laughter fades as I realize
why she had been arrested
in the first place.

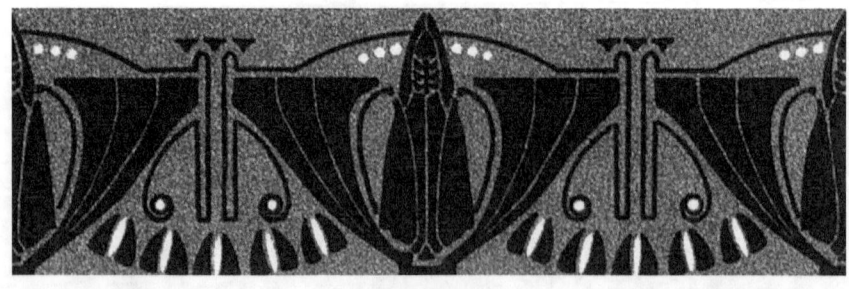

About Polk Street and *The Polk Street Review* anthology

The Polk Street Review (TPSR) is a unique creative place-making project that has received international status with submissions and followers from all over the world. The project's annual anthology is published by *Community • Education • Arts Press*, a division of *Community • Education • Arts*, a 501c3 nonprofit Arts organization based in Noblesville, IN that has a global perspective. TPSR is a one-of-a-kind anthology dedicated to publishing prose, poetry, song lyrics, and artwork images submitted by professional and amateur creatives from anywhere in the world.

The Polk Street Review book is named in honor of a significant historic Noblesville street originally named after William Conner's partner, Josiah Polk. Mills were at the north end of the street, and the old courthouse, bars, liveries, hotels, homes, and other buildings of industry lined its southern stretch. Polk Street is now called 8th Street.

The street dates to 1823 when Noblesville was laid out; it is the north/south road that used to have railroad tracks running alongside and down the middle of it. The historic Heritage Railway tracks were removed by the City of Noblesville a few years ago, and trains that ran through Noblesville for almost 200 years are gone forever.

At some point in Noblesville's history, Polk Street became the dividing line between white-collar and blue-collar neighborhoods, white and black neighborhoods, residential and industrial areas, and high ground *versus* the flood plain. Over time those divisions became so ingrained that people didn't mention them, but they "knew" them. Social and economic division are like that: they take on a life of their own unless we consciously resist them, because they become taken for granted, like history itself. A lot of folks today see 8th Street as just a main route through town, but the old road represents the history of Noblesville, her businesses, and the generations who lived here.

Noblesville continues to see a lot of change as developers have their way, but we believe it can retain some of its unique historic small-town qualities while recognizing that certain areas, certain landmarks, and certain streets are playing a part in the City's vision for the future. In today's developer-driven world, we hope that Noblesville can remain both a home to artistic souls and a special place with a small-town feel.

Our annual anthology project, *The Polk Street Review*, celebrates heritage, history, and people in submissions of original prose, poetry, song lyrics, and artwork images. In the past, we asked that either the subject matter or the submitter have a connection to Noblesville, but as our organization has grown a global audience we've opened submissions to a diverse global arts community.

You may wonder about the grasshopper in the original TPSR logo:

We often refer to our contributors as *grasshoppers* and to the people who quietly support them as *ants*. These insect references are taken from Aesop's fable, *The Ant & The Grasshopper*. Grasshoppers are the dreamers, the creatives: we artists, writers, and musicians. Ants are support us: our hardworking loved ones toiling away in the background. Grasshoppers create that which feeds the soul; ants create that which feeds the body.

The world needs both ants and grasshoppers, so cheers to both!

David Allen is a retired journalist who worked on newspapers in New York, Virginia, Indiana, and the Far East. He is a former vice president and contest director for the Poetry Society of Indiana. Allen has four books of poetry for sale on Amazon. Visit his blog at www.davidallen.nu.

Donavan Barrier is a poet residing in La Porte, Indiana. After competing in 2012 at the Chicago Youth Poetry Festival Louder Than a Bomb, he got the poetry bug. Since then, Donavan's performed his poetry at the South Bend Civil Rights Center and won first place in undergraduate poetry at the 2018 Stark-Tinkham contest at Purdue Northwest. He graduated in 2019 from PNW with a BA in Communications.

Vivianne Belle lives in Noblesville; she enjoys occasionally writing poetry and prose.

JAC, aka John A. Caviness, grew up in Noblesville, graduating from Noblesville High School, and received a Bachelor of Arts in Foreign Languages (German Studies) and Master of Science from the *Center for Communication and Information Sciences* (CICS) at Ball State University. John loves to fix problems, ease frustration, and optimize quality of life while working with technology. He helps the company he works for, and their clients, thrive in the modern technological landscape. John is creative and occasionally known to enjoy some odd songs and shows with a Mead in hand. He started using JAC when he started writing poetry with friends Z. Rose and B. Monét. John's been a male ally to women and other disenfranchised groups throughout his life, and helps diverse people work together in the technology arena.

Alys Caviness-Gober is a disabled anthropologist, self-taught artist, and writer. She taught Anthropology, Women's Studies, and ESOL at university level and was a PhD candidate in Applied Linguistics until her disabilities worsened. In 2011, Alys was juried into *Hamilton County Artists' Association* (photography; 2D). She and author Sarah E. Morin cofounded an annual literature-based project, *Noblesville Interdisciplinary Creativity Expo* (NICE). In 2014, Alys founded *Community • Education • Arts* (CEArts), an all-volunteer

501(c)(3) Arts organization; it hosts NICE and publishes an annual anthology, *The Polk Street Review*. As a FY2017 Indiana Arts Commission *Individual Artist Project* Grant Award recipient, Alys created a series of large-scale paintings expressing life with hidden disabilities. She was selected for IUPUI Arts and Humanities Institute's *Religion Spirituality, and the Arts* 2018/19 Seminar Class, is included in *INverse: Indiana's Poetry Archive*, served on the Noblesville Arts Council, and is a member of *Noble Poets* and *Poetry Society of Indiana*. Alys' poetry has been in global anthologies since the 1980s, in the *Last Stanza Poetry Journal*, *The Polk Street Review*, and in her own poetry/artwork collections, *Naked In Wonderland (Vols I, II, III, IV)*. Alys' artwork, photographs, and poetry have received national and international recognition.

Kenneth Conklin retired from many years as a technical writer for IBM and other firms, and was a feature writer for a newspaper in Colorado. His poetry and short stories appeared in a regional magazine in Kentucky. After Ken's wife Katy had her second stroke, they moved to Fishers IN to be closer to their daughter and her family. Katy passed away last year after complications from lupus after heart surgery.

Jeff Couch has lived everywhere from Colorado to the Canary Islands. His piece in this year's TPSR was inspired by personal history and time spent in Spain. Jeff resides in Indiana with his family and their beloved dog. He's working on perfecting his Spanish hot chocolate recipe and releasing his first book, a novel of interconnected children's stories. You can read his blog at Couchsview.blogspot.com and find his Facebook page at Facebook.com/Quillnib.

Jerry Dreesen is a self-taught artist and poet. He loves to challenge himself in a variety of art styles and mediums, including watercolor, acrylics, pastels, and experiments in clay modeling and found sculptures. Jerry is a member of Nickel Plate Arts and the online gallery, Plogix. He's exhibited work in many art and business venues. Jerry's art has sold throughout the US, Great Britain, Europe, and Japan.

Alison Harlos has finally been spending time rediscovering her creative side. She lives in Old Town with her husband, 3 offspring, and 3 doggos. She finds joy in her family (obviously), singing, wound care, being outside, talking in weird voices, and snuggling with her pups.

John R Hinton is an Indiana poet and writer. His writing is inspired by our daily human interactions and the accompanying emotions: love, hate, indifference, passion. His words explore who we are, how we behave. Sometimes eloquent, other times gritty, these words seek to reveal the joy and pain of this beautiful human existence. He is the author of two poetry collections: *Blackbird Songs* and *Held*. John is the President of Poetry Society of Indiana and a member of Last Stanza Poetry Association.

Chuck Kellum began writing poetry while a senior in college studying engineering and wrote about 120 poems over a dozen years before getting married, but then was too busy after that with work and family. His writing of poems on a somewhat frequent basis resumed in 2009 after he was no longer working full time. He's been a member of the Noble Poets poetry club since 2017

Dr. Leah Leach is the founder and Executive Director of the *Gal's Guide Library*, the first women's history lending library in the United States. Before founding Gal's Guide in 2018, she ran a successful film company, winning 12 cinematic awards. Leah has won six production awards for podcasts; listen in weekly as the *Gal's Guide Podcast* talks about cool women of history. Leah is a writer and mixed media artist, teaches a fall writing program, and is a judge for the *Gal's Guide Anthology*. Visit her at leah-leach.com and galsguide.org

🌐 **Mairéad Lewis** (pr. *mih-rayd loo-whis*) is a Celtic writer and artist living in Dublin, Ireland.

Dorothy Lorant is a retired Vice President of Public Relations & Advertising of a Fortune 500 company. She began her career in journalism in 1957 as a reporter for *The Boston Globe*.

Mona Mehas (she/her) writes about growing up poor, accumulating grief, and climate change. Mona has used the pseudonym Patience Young. She is a retired, disabled teacher in Indiana, spending most days at her laptop with two old cats as chaperones. Mona's published essays, stories, and poetry in journals, anthologies, and two museums.

In 2020, Mona watched every *Star Trek* show and movie in chronological order. Follow on Twitter @Patienc77732097 and linktr.ee/monaiv.

Sarah E. Morin serves as a kidwrangler at Conner Prairie, a history museum in Fishers, Indiana. She's published two books, *Waking Beauty* (a Christian fantasy novel based on *Sleeping Beauty*) and *Rapunzel the Hairbrained*, a children's picture book that forms the basis of a workshop to build girls' self-esteem. Sarah E. is the Premier Poet of Poetry Society of Indiana, Secretary of *Community Education Arts*, and co-founder of *Noblesville Interdisciplinary Creativity Expo* (NICE). She loved the years she spent living above the Clock Shop in Noblesville, and remains engaged in the downtown scene through Noble Poets (new poets welcome – 3rd Tuesday each month at 6:30pm in Zoom). When she grows up, she wants to be a child prodigy. Visit her at sarahemorin.com.

Noble Poets is a Noblesville, IN area poetry group affiliated with the state of Indiana's official poetry organization, Poetry Society of Indiana.

Mike Nierste's poetry is published in poetry journals and anthologies including; *Flying Island, Tipton Poetry Journal, frogpond, The Polk Street Review, Cowboys & Cocktails - Poetry from the True Grit Saloon, Haiku for Hikers, and Reflections on Little Eagle Creek.* He has poems in Indiana Arts Council's online collection *INverse*. Mike is the author of a book of contradictory quotes and contranyms titled *Contra-Diction*, and the poetry books; *Savor, Discoveries, and Still Waters*.

Jean Roberts is a retired plant scientist who lives in the country in northern Hamilton County, where she grows wonderful flowers. She is also a guitar player and band leader. Jean volunteers at the Pioneer Village at the Indiana State Fair.

Patricia Rossi is an avid runner and writer, currently living in New York. Her written pieces, narrative essays, poems, and academic history articles have been published in newspapers, magazines, literary journals, and academic textbooks.

Bonita Cox Searle is a frequent contributor of poetry, creative nonfiction, and fiction to *The Polk Street Review*. She has also contributed poetry to the *Last Stanza Poetry Journal* series, F*lying Island*, and *The Indiana Voice Journal*. Bonnie lives in Noblesville, Indiana with her husband. She has no cats, no dogs, and no pet parakeets, but she does live by a pond full of herons, ducks, geese, and noisy frogs.

🌐 **Ndaba Sibanda** is a Bulawayo-born poet, novelist, thought leader and nonfiction writer who has authored twenty-eight published books of various genres and persuasions and coauthored more than 100 published books. Ndaba's works are in *Page & Spine, Piker Press, SCARLET LEAF REVIEW, Universidad Complutense de Madrid, the Pangolin Review, Kalahari Review, Botsotso, The Ofi Press Magazine, Hawaii Pacific Review, Deltona Howl, The song is, JONAH magazine, The Polk Street Review, Poetry Potion, Saraba Magazine, The Borfski Press, East Coast Literary Review,* and *Whispering Prairie Press*. He's received the following nominations: National Arts Merit Awards (NAMA), the Mary Ballard Poetry Chapbook Prize, the Best of the Net Prose, and the Pushcart Prize. Ndaba's book *Notes, Themes, Things And Other Things: Confronting Controversies, Contradictions And Indoctrinations* was considered for *The 2019 Restless Book Prize for New Immigrant Writing in Nonfiction*. Ndaba's book titled *Cabinet Meetings: Of Big And Small Preys* was considered for *The Graywolf Press Africa Prize 2018*.

Nancy Simmonds writes letters, postcards, and poems from northeastern Indiana. She is a member of the Poetry Society of Indiana and of the NIPoets local poetry group, as well as a longtime member of a university book group. When a pen isn't in her hand or her head in a book, Nancy designs and sews scrap quilts and designs paper collage art, plans travel adventures, and runs in local Fort Wayne Running Club events and in virtual races for bling and bragging rights.

Rue Sparks is an amalgamation of neurosis and nonsense held together by duct tape and sheer stubbornness. A widow, disabled, and a member of the queer community, they traverse the equally harsh and cathartic landscape where trauma and healing align to create stories that burrow into the hearts and minds of their readers. In addition to *The Stars Will Guide Us Back*, Sparks has authored the novella

Daylight Chasers, and the contemporary mystery novel *The Fable of Wren*. They volunteer as the Communications Coordinator at the women's library, *Gal's Guide to the Galaxy*, and as an artist for the indie publisher, *Lost Boys Press*. They live in Noblesville, Indiana in the USA with their sweet senior support dog and cantankerous cat.

Marilyn J Wolf lives in Fishers, IN, and has been writing since childhood with varying rates of success and support. Nonetheless, the writing has continued. Internationally acclaimed *In Celebration of the Death of Faeries* is her first chapbook. Presently, she is editing a second. (When is a piece of writing ever "done?" 😜 Once that determination is  made, it will be published.) Her work has been published in *The Polk Street Review, Last Stanza Poetry Journal, Haiku journal, Poet's Choice*, and *Living Artistically*; displayed in galleries at Nickel Plate Arts, Community Education Arts Online Showcase, Lost Dog Gallery, and the INverse Poetry Archive. She writes regularly in a variety of publications on Medium.com at https://medium.com/@Wolfen25. Marilyn is a member of local, state, and national poetry organizations, and currently serves as the First Vice President of Poetry Society of Indiana.

About *Community • Education • Arts, Inc.*

Community • Education • Arts, Inc. (CEArts) is a 501(c)(3) nonprofit Arts organization that is based in Noblesville with a global reach. Our organization is run by three dedicated people volunteering their time so that CEArts can continue to host online exhibits on our website, record @theroundtable arts podcast, and our two annual projects: the classic literature-based project, *Noblesville Interdisciplinary Creativity Expo* (NICE), and *The Polk Street Review* project. A special *thank you* to our volunteer CEArts Board Officers:

President: Alys Caviness-Gober
Secretary: Sarah E. Morin
Treasurer: Joyce Perry

The Polk Street Review is published by
Community • Education • Arts Press
a division of
Community • Education • Arts, Inc.
Noblesville, IN 46060
CEArts.org
info@cearts.org